HIKING THE CATSKILLS

HELP US KEEP THIS GUIDE UP TO DATE

Every effort has been made by the authors and editors to make this guide as accurate and useful as possible. However, many things can change after a guide is published—trails are rerouted, regulations change, facilities come under new management, and so forth.

We would love to hear from you concerning your experiences with this guide and how you feel it could be improved and kept up to date. While we may not be able to respond to all comments and suggestions, we'll take them to heart, and we'll also make certain to share them with the authors. Please send your comments and suggestions to editorial@GlobePequot.com.

Thanks for your input, and happy trails!

Catch views of the Berkshire Mountains, the Hudson River, the Ashokan Reservoir, and the Shawangunk and Catskill Mountains from the firetower. (Hike 12)

HIKING THE CATSKILLS

A GUIDE TO THE AREA'S GREATEST HIKES

Randi Minetor and Stacey Freed

FALCONGUIDES

ESSEX, CONNECTICUT

FALCONGUIDES®

An imprint of Globe Pequot, the trade division of
The Rowman & Littlefield Publishing Group, Inc.
4501 Forbes Blvd., Ste. 200
Lanham, MD 20706
www.rowman.com

Falcon and FalconGuides are registered trademarks and Make Adventure Your Story is a
trademark of The Rowman & Littlefield Publishing Group, Inc.

Distributed by NATIONAL BOOK NETWORK

Photos by Nic Minetor and Jeff Thompson unless otherwise noted
Maps by Melissa Baker, The Rowman & Littlefield Publishing Group, Inc.

British Library Cataloguing in Publication Information available

Library of Congress Cataloging-in-Publication Data

Names: Minetor, Randi author. | Freed, Stacey, author.
Title: Hiking the Catskills : a guide to the area's greatest hikes / Randi Minetor and Stacey Freed.
Description: Guilford, Connecticut : FalconGuides, [2022] | Includes index. | Summary: "A guide
   to 40 of the best hikes among the Catskills' famous peaks above 3,500 feet, as well as more
   moderate trails to backcountry waterfalls, easier trails to some of the area's most spectacular
   viewpoints, and rail trails that provide access to woodlands and unusual geological wonders"
   — Provided by publisher.
Identifiers: LCCN 2021061249 (print) | LCCN 2021061250 (ebook) | ISBN 9781493063000
   (Paperback : acid-free paper) | ISBN 9781493062997 (ePub)
Subjects: LCSH: Hiking—New York (State)—Catskill Mountains—Guidebooks. | Walking—New York
   (State)—Catskill Mountains—Guidebooks. | Trails—New York (State)—Catskill Mountains—
   Guidebooks. | Rail-trails—New York (State)—Catskill Mountains—Guidebooks. | Waterfalls—
   New York (State)—Catskill Mountains—Guidebooks. | Catskill Mountains (N.Y.)—Description and
   travel. | Catskill Mountains (N.Y.)—Guidebooks.
Classification: LCC GV199.42.N652 M564 2022 (print) | LCC GV199.42.N652 (ebook) | DDC
   796.5109747—dc23/eng/20220224
LC record available at https://lccn.loc.gov/2021061249
LC ebook record available at https://lccn.loc.gov/2021061250

♾️ The paper used in this publication meets the minimum requirements of American National
Standard for Information Sciences—Permanence of Paper for Printed Library Materials, ANSI/
NISO Z39.48-1992.

CONTENTS

THE HIKES

Northeastern Catskills   *1*

Northwestern Catskills   *80*

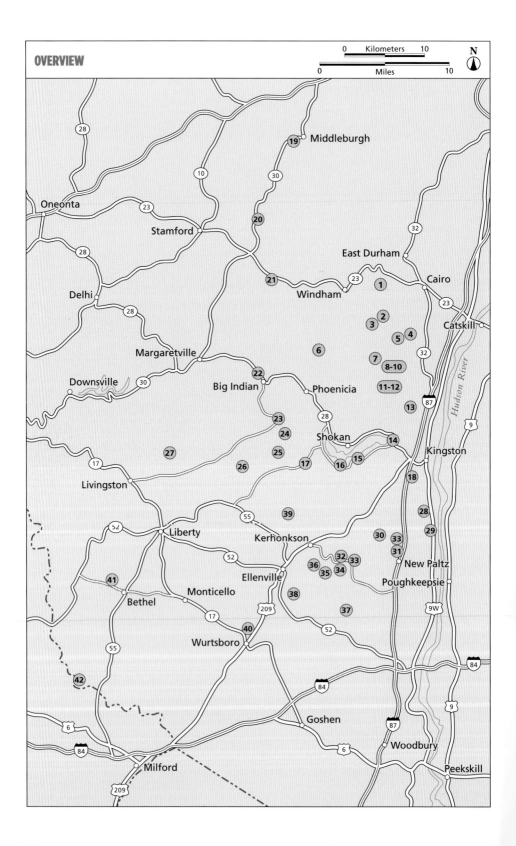

ACKNOWLEDGMENTS

STACEY

First and foremost, I have to thank my coauthor for giving me the opportunity to work on this book. It gave me the kick in the pants I needed to explore a place I'd always wanted to visit. I'd also like to thank my sons, Henry and Lucas Erbland, and my dad, Goody Freed, for their support and encouragement. And, of course, thanks to my husband, Jeff Thompson, who documented our journey in photos. He also never let me run out of water.

This book would not have been possible without the help of friends, in particular Jeff Graf, who directed us to the most interesting trails, kept us from getting lost, and whose knowledge added nuanced layers to my understanding of the region. Thank you, too, to Abbie Duchon and Gregg St. Clair for sharing their home and local knowledge. I am the luckiest person, with lots of people on Team Stacey: Heidi Skolnik, Heidi Kaufman, Drew Dubrin, Theresa and Harvey Beldner, Renee Beerman, Rachel Gordon, Hinda Mandell, Kris Thieme, Maria Murillo, Howard Solomon, Robin Flanigan, Judy Miller, Gary and Lisa Freed, Colleen Smith, Kathi Mooney, Pam Bartell, Lucille Kelly, and Ellen Smith. To them I offer my gratitude for their time, energy, and listening skills.

None of our treks would be possible without the amazing work of the many professionals and volunteers who maintain the Catskills trails. Thank you, thank you to the New York–New Jersey Trail Conference and the folks at the Catskills Visitor Center for keeping this region accessible.

RANDI

It is always my pleasure to work with the crack team at Falcon Guides, from the inception of each project with editorial director David Legere to the production team, including production editor Meredith Dias, copy editor Paulette Baker, layout artist Melissa Evarts, proofreader Ann Seifert, and cartographer Melissa Baker. Our hiking trip to the Catskills was our first venture out of town as the first COVID-19 lockdown lifted, so I am even more grateful than usual for the excuse to leave the house, pack up the car, and head into the hills.

Ever in my corner (and now in Stacey's as well), my agent Regina Ryan took care of the financial and legal aspects of this partnership with her usual aplomb. I so appreciate her careful supervision of this part of my career.

No hike, no trip, and no resulting book can be complete without the participation and photography of my husband, Nic Minetor, who trekked all these trails with me under some of the most complex, socially distanced conditions we've encountered. I rely not only on his good judgment and preparedness on trails, but also on his sense of direction; who knows where I would be if he were not by my side.

The view from Catskill Mountain House inspired many writers and artists.

To the friends who support my every step—Ken Horowitz and Rose-Anne Moore, Lisa Jaccoma, Kevin Hyde, Martha and Peter Schermerhorn, Ruth Watson and John King, neighbor Pam Bartemus (who mowed our lawn while we were gone, for heaven's sake), Cindy Blair, Lorraine Woerner, and cousins Paula and Rich Landis—I thank you for keeping me grounded in all circumstances, whether weird or wonderful.

And finally, to my writing partner, Stacey Freed: Thank you so much for taking on the highest mountains and delivering on every promise. I would have had to pass on this project without you; you not only made it a far less taxing journey for me but also maintained your good nature from start to finish. Bravo!

The newly refurbished Catskills Visitor Center in Mount Tremper.

MEET YOUR GUIDES

RANDI MINETOR

Finally, the Catskills! What a pleasure it was to spend some quality time in this region for my sixth book that includes hikes in this area. It's been twelve years since *Best Easy Day Hikes: Hudson River Valley* was published, and since then my husband, photographer Nic Minetor, and I have explored parts of the Catskills while working on the first and second editions of *Hiking Waterfalls in New York*, as well as *Day Trips in the Hudson Valley, Hiking the Lower Hudson River Valley*, and *Hiking Through History New York*. This is the first time we've focused on all the bounty the Catskills can offer, and we are eager to direct you to our favorite hikes throughout the five-county area.

I've loved hiking since I was a Girl Scout back in the 1960s—and now, at age 63, I know that hiking is a key factor in staying healthy. Still, I had to be judicious in choosing the hikes in this book, as some health issues keep me from hiking at higher elevations or scrambling up big rock faces. So I'm delighted to introduce my coauthor of this book, Stacey Freed, who took on the peaks above 3,500 feet. You'll find plenty to challenge you in these pages, but you'll also discover some fairly easy hikes that may not have come to your attention before.

STACEY FREED

As a writer, I spend most of my workday at a desk. But I make it a priority to get outside to walk, run, or hike every day. Motion is meditative; it helps me think.

I typically write about the built world—design, remodeling, construction, architecture, real estate and housing issues—for a variety of national consumer and trade publications. When Randi asked me to take on some of the more strenuous hikes and cowrite this book, I jumped at the chance—admittedly with some trepidation.

The Catskills seemed daunting. As people will tell you, there are "easy" hikes and there are "easy hikes for the Catskills." I was worried. But my husband, Jeff, and I were able to hike every mile of every hike, and every single hike left us breathless—in a good way, in awe of the beauty of the region. I hope this book inspires you to get out and explore.

SIX HIKING TIPS

Hiking in the Catskills has a special set of challenges. Here are our tips for staying safe, healthy, and upright on the region's trails.

1. **Carry a stick.** You'll find it much easier to make your way up and down rock-strewn trails if you use a walking stick or trekking poles.

2. **Dress against ticks.** Ticks that carry Lyme disease are a serious infestation in this area. Long sleeves, long pants, and plenty of insect repellent will help keep you safe.

3. **Be mindful of bears.** We saw black bears on every trip we made to the Catskills. Chances are you may spot one at a safe distance. To keep from having close-up encounters, make noise as you hike, and have your bear spray at the ready.

4. **Remember to eat.** You may not feel hungry, but when you lose energy halfway up a steep trail, a handy granola bar will restore your drive.

5. **Use a compass.** Electronic devices can tell you which way is north, but there's no cellular or wireless service on many of these trails. Learn to orient yourself with an actual compass. If you've never used one, get out on an easy trail and practice before you take on something harder.

6. **Pack it out.** Don't join others in spoiling the Catskill wilderness. Take your trash with you—and if you can, pick up after others.

TOP SIX HIKES

1. **Huckleberry Point Trail:** There aren't many easy trails in the Catskills, but almost anyone at any skill level will enjoy this hike that meanders across streams and around fields of mountain laurel and offers a grand view at the summit. It will whet your appetite for more Catskills hiking.

2. **Bonticou Crag:** The most difficult rock scramble you can do without ropes. The hike presents this great challenge, but it also offers a path around the boulders. Either way up results in sweeping views of the north and west Catskill Range.

3. **Dibble's Quarry:** If you're looking for a good hike to take the kids on, this is it. Not too long, not too strenuous, and it ends with bluestone thrones fit for giants.

4. **Red Hill Fire Tower:** A relatively easy hike with the chance to experience one of only five remaining fire towers in the Catskills. Plan on getting there around lunchtime; hang out at the picnic tables and chat with the ranger, who can answer all your questions.

5. **Gertrude's Nose/Minnewaska Trail:** There's no word other than "breathtaking" to describe this hike; it's one of the most scenic views of the Shawangunk Mountains. The hike is plenty challenging as you occasionally walk along the narrow ridge and cross crevasses, but the payoff is worth it.

6. **Overlook Mountain:** A little history. A little romance. Now in ruins, the once-grand Overlook Mountain House hotel is a testament to how well-loved this region is. Artists, thinkers, writers, philosophers, statesmen—all found inspiration here.

WELCOME TO THE CATSKILLS

If all you know about the Catskills comes from the movie *Dirty Dancing* or an episode of *The Marvelous Mrs. Maisel*, you are in for an exciting surprise.

The days of the structured summer resort experience are long gone, but the Catskills continue to provide a paradise to lovers of outdoor sports—particularly anglers, who come from around the world to fish its rivers. And its wealth of wild forests, wilderness areas, state and national preserves, and manageable mountain summits attract hikers at every level, from first-timers to experienced rock climbers.

Today the Catskills draw 12 million tourists every year to vacation and explore, supporting some 18,500 jobs and generating $1.3 billion in revenue for the region's hotels, restaurants, stores, and other businesses. But even with these visitation levels, there is plenty of wilderness to go around. Popular trails like Kaaterskill Falls and Bonticou Crag may have jammed parking lots on weekends from June through October, but visitors can use this book to find a wide selection of hiking options that offer their own visual delights, from secluded ponds and wetlands to ledges with unobstructed mountain views.

It wasn't always like this. The history of the Catskills spans centuries of dispute, development, industry, art, and resort life, all of which shaped the region's current offerings to visitors and residents.

The result of continental drift followed by the moving ice sheets of the Wisconsin glaciation (about 75,000 to 11,000 years ago), the Catskills are part of the Appalachian Mountains, a range that runs from Newfoundland and Labrador in Canada to central Alabama. These ancient peaks received much of their sediments from the erosion of the Acadian Mountains to the east, a process that finally ended about 325 million years ago. The sediments settled, condensed, and formed solid rock, with an upper layer of softer sediment that the glaciers scoured away. The peaks you see now get their gentle, undulating appearance

The Catskills' forests were nearly lost to industry in the nineteenth century.

Bluestone Wild Forest provides open views of Onteora Lake.

(at least at a distance) from these massive events of moving earth and sliding ice. Rocky Mountain enthusiasts may scoff at what we Northeasterners consider "peaks," but those western mountains are children compared with these grandparents of geologic time.

Humans are the Johnny-come-latelies in this region, arriving as recently as a few hundred years ago. The Esopus tribe, a segment of the Lenape nation, found their way to Ulster and Sullivan Counties from farther south in Pennsylvania and Delaware, living in small communities and keeping much to themselves. A series of land sales to colonists from Europe pulled them into direct conflict with Dutch settlers, however, and soon they were embroiled in what became known as the Esopus Wars. When four years of battles ended in 1663, the Esopus sold much of their land to Huguenots, a French religious sect that settled in what is now New Paltz. Smallpox did in many of the tribe's remaining members, and the rest moved on to western New York and farther north into Canada.

The first European name to become indelibly associated with the region was Johannes Hardenbergh, a land speculator who petitioned the British government in 1706 for a grant to purchase a large section of the area. It took Hardenbergh and his partner, Jacob Rutsen, two years of haggling with the governor to clinch the deal, but once the papers were signed, they had managed to claim title to 2 million acres—nearly all of what we now know as the Catskills. The shady deal tied up the land for decades, the lack of any kind of actual survey preventing its settlement. Farmers and tribes other than the Esopus claimed that the land actually belonged to them, and other speculators attempted to carve out pieces for themselves. In the end, the Revolutionary War settled everyone's claims by making the land the property of the United States.

The opening of the Catskill Mountain House in 1824 near the summit of Kaaterskill High Peak signaled a new era for the region, introducing the concept of tourism to the uncommonly beautiful area. The high-class hotel stood in what is now North–South Lake Park, overlooking the Hudson Valley and both North and South Lakes, and the views from its many windows and verandas attracted all manner of moneyed visitors. The artists of the Hudson River School, America's first uniquely regional style of landscape painting, found it particularly inspiring. Thomas Cole, considered the father of the Hudson River School, frequented the establishment and spent several seasons painting from its front yard and gardens. Novelist Washington Irving spent time there gathering inspiration for his own works. The Mountain House's popularity with the wealthy and in-the-know expanded further in 1839 when Charles Beach purchased and remodeled the property. Soon other opulent hotels sprang up in the same general area—most of them easier to reach, as a trip up Kaaterskill High Peak's 1,600-foot incline to the Mountain House took as much as 5 hours by stagecoach. The Mountain House suffered another blow when it turned out that Kaaterskill, at 3,655 feet in elevation, was not the highest mountain in the Catskills—4,180-foot Slide Mountain beat it handily. It continued to entertain many guests into the 1900s but closed in 1941; the state conservation department demolished it in 1963.

Other hotels continued to flourish, however, even as other industries began to dominate the region. New York and Pennsylvania worked together to build a canal system through Sullivan and Ulster Counties to reach the Hudson River, the most efficient route to bring anthracite coal out of the lower state to market in New York City. With the canal to transport goods and forests filled with hemlock—the bark of which contains strong tannins, used in tanning animal hides—the leathermaking industry took hold, and entire forests fell to its will. When the region ran out of hemlock, enterprising individuals discovered that the sun-loving hardwoods that grew where hemlocks once stood could also be harvested for distillation—this time for the acids within their wood, which were necessary for making wool cloth and other products. Bluestone quarrying stripped away rock walls to bring paving stone to city sidewalks in New York City, Albany, and well beyond. It looked as though the Catskills landscape would be damaged forever by one industry's needs after another.

Luckily, another kind of financial concern won out. In a bid to avoid paying a large property tax debt to New York State, two state assemblymen from Ulster County lobbied hard to pass the Forest Preserve Act, which turned much of the Catskills' 700,000 acres into protected land. In 1894, this act became Article 14 in the state's revised constitution, guaranteeing that most of Catskill Park would remain forever wild, surrounded by the "Blue Line" boundary that sealed its protection.

Article 14 could be breached, however. Just eleven years later, New York City turned to the Catskills when it needed reservoirs to provide clean water to its inhabitants. A number of small Catskill towns were sacrificed for the endeavor, with land claims that tied up courts for decades, but the result was the Ashokan and Schoharie Reservoirs and a spectacular feat of engineering to bring their pure water to the nation's largest metropolis. Three trails in this book take advantage of the scenic and historical treasures offered by Ashokan Reservoir.

In the 1920s, a trend that had been in progress for some time took hold in earnest. Jewish immigrants, living in tenements on Manhattan's Lower East Side and throughout the five boroughs, discovered that boardinghouses and summer camps in Sullivan and Ulster Counties offered things they could not get in the stifling city: fresh air, fresh food, lovely scenery, and fellowship with other Jews from eastern Europe. Jews often found themselves the targets of discrimination and exclusion in cities, forbidden from shopping, eating, or socializing with people of other descents. Hearing that the Catskills welcomed them with open arms, they made their way north and filled hotels, camps, bungalows, and other rental properties throughout the summer. These establishments catered specifi- cally to the needs of Jewish people, offering kosher food, comfortable accommodations, and entertainment in their native languages. Subsequent generations of Jews enjoyed luxury hotels like Grossinger's, the Concord, the Nevele, and Kutcher's, to name the most famous, and entertainment including the finest comedians of the 1940s through the 1970s: Woody Allen, Milton Berle, Joey Bishop, Sid Caesar, Billy Crystal, Rodney Dangerfield, Gabe Kaplan, Jerry Lewis, Jackie Mason, Joan Rivers, Jerry Seinfeld, Henny Youngman, and many others.

By the mid-1960s, however, the "Borscht Belt" resorts had begun to decline as barriers to Jewish inclusion finally fell. A new generation of young adults felt more assimilated to American culture than their parents and grandparents had, and they saw less need to segregate from the rest of the population for their summer pleasure. Some of the largest resorts struggled on into the 1980s and 1990s, but the last of them—the Concord—shut- tered in 1998.

Today's visitors enjoy a different Catskills experience, one with a decidedly more adventurous appeal. Thousands of miles of hiking trails crisscross Catskill Park, including 6,000 acres of state recreation areas with campgrounds and spots for skiing, fishing, boat- ing, and swimming. A splendid 130,000 acres are designated as "Wild Forest," perfect for hiking, camping, cross-country skiing, mountain biking, snowmobiling, and horseback riding. It's in the 143,000 acres of wilderness areas like Windham-Blackhead Range, Indian Head, Hunter–West Kill, Slide Mountain, and Big Indian that many hikers find recreation and solitude, as there are no motor vehicles or bicycles allowed.

This book can offer only a sampling of the bounty you can discover here, so we present some of the most popular hikes in the region, some of the newer and lesser-known ones, and some unique places you should not miss. You will find high peaks and low valleys, tough ascents and easy strolls, and just about all the scenery you can handle.

WEATHER

Few places can match New York State for its gorgeous spring and summer, when flowers scent the air, leaves embrace the trees with intense emerald shades, and the sky turns cobalt to complement the sunlight. The sun shines six days out of ten from June through August, and while spring temperatures can linger in the 50s and 60s until June, idyllic summer days average in the 70s and 80s, with occasional spikes into the 90s in June or July, and cooler temperatures at night. Heavy rains often arrive in April, although they rarely last more than a day or two at a time. The Catskills have no dry season, so be prepared for rain any time you visit.

To truly appreciate the transformation to vibrant spring and summer seasons in upstate New York, however, we must face the area's legendary winters. Winter temperatures average in the mid-20s, with significant dips into the teens and below in January, February, and March. Check the "windchill" before making a winter hike—especially at altitude—as the air can feel much colder than the temperature indicates. The annual late-January or early-February thaw can push temperatures into the 50s for a few days, but the cold will return, usually lasting on and off into late March. Snow is guaranteed—an average Catskill winter has about 50 inches, although not all at once; snow accumulation on the higher peaks can reach 100 to 120 inches. Check your selected park's website before attempting any winter hike—the trail may be impassable after a heavy snow, or the road to the trailhead may be closed.

The Catskills enjoy a high percentage of sunny days—as much as 67 percent in summer; nearly 40 percent even in the doldrums of winter. Cloudy days can make for exciting photos from mountain summits or open fields, however, so don't rule out your hike just because the day is overcast. On any day when sun is likely, be sure to wear sunscreen, especially if you're heading up to a summit or you expect to spend time on an open rock face.

Crisp fall days highlight colorful foliage in the Shawangunk Valley.

Fall equals spring in its spectacle, with days in the 50s and 60s, bright blue skies, and foliage panoramas throughout the area's parks and preserves. The emerald hillsides turn shades of orange, gold, and crimson in fall, making the trails to mountain summits some of the most popular places in the state. If you're planning to hike to see fall foliage, go on a weekday if possible, or hit the trail early in the day. By afternoon, you may have more company than you will enjoy.

FLORA AND FAUNA

The Catskills offer a rich diversity of plant, bird, animal, and insect species, most of which mean you no harm at all. There's something interesting going on just about anywhere you look, and most of what you see requires nothing more than a keen eye and a perceptive ear to identify.

Forest floors may be carpeted with mayapple and marsh marigold in spring, and then give way to large areas of rattlesnake, evergreen grape, royal, and other ferns. You may see the tiny white flowers of bunchberry growing along forest trails, producing clusters of bright red berries in summer. Tall stalks of yellow and white sweet clover dominate the edges of greenways and rail trails in spring and early summer, while the bright purple and white blooms of dame's rocket overtake fields throughout spring, especially in areas close to water. The flowers of such invasive shrubs as multiflora rose and Tatarian honeysuckle add their intoxicating scents to the clear spring air in forests and along the edges of field trails.

Open meadows and grassy mountainsides become vast expanses of nodding wildflowers in summer, with coneflower, black-eyed Susan, butterfly milkweed, bee balm, common milkweed, blazing star, common fleabane, and joe-pye weed among the most familiar native blooms. A wide variety of invasive, non-native flowering plants are mixed in as well, including purple loosestrife, oxeye daisy, garlic mustard, chicory, bindweed,

Fields of coneflower and black-eyed Susan emerge in summer.

black swallow-wort, and several less-aggressive species. Marshes may be filled with tall marsh grasses called phragmites (or common reed), which sport a tassel at the top of a long stalk. Some calm pond surfaces host lily pads and white or yellow water lilies.

Not all plants are friendly. Poison ivy can be found along many trails; keep an eye out for shiny green "leaves of three" and do as the rhyme says: "Let it be." Poison ivy also climbs trees, so before you put out a hand to steady yourself against a tree trunk, look to be sure it isn't wrapped in a suspicious vine. (Virginia creeper also climbs trees and looks similar to poison ivy, but it has five leaves instead of three.)

CRITTERS

You will see many animals as you hike, with gray and red squirrels and eastern chipmunks the most frequent trail companions. White-tailed deer are easy to spot ahead of you on a trail or from a distance as you pass a field. While you will see considerable evidence of beaver activity along lakes and ponds in heavily forested areas, you're not likely to see the creatures themselves at work unless you hike early in the morning or close to dusk. Coyotes, red foxes, porcupines, and raccoons are all residents of the region and may put in an appearance.

Black bears, while not common, are a distinct possibility in the Catskills. We saw bear scat on several trails, and we spotted young bears foraging among berry bushes on a number of occasions. Take the necessary precautions to avoid startling, or being startled by, a bear:

- **Make noise when hiking.** Bears have only average hearing and rather poor eyesight. Make plenty of noise when you're hiking—talk, sing, call out, and clap your hands at regular intervals. Bear bells generally are not loud enough to let the animals know you're on your way. Once a bear hears you coming, chances are good that it will move away from the trail and leave you alone.

- **Assume that bears are nearby.** Even the most popular and well-used trails may go through bear country, so don't assume there are no bears on heavily populated trails. Keep making noise (and ignore the people who give you the evil eye for being noisy), and keep your eyes open for bears in the area.

- **Watch out for surprises.** When you approach streams, shrubs full of berries, fields of cow parsnip, or areas of dense vegetation, keep your eyes open for bears. As they can't always smell or hear you, you may startle a bear by arriving quietly.

Black bears want nothing to do with you, so make noise to let them know you're coming.

- **Do not approach bears.** Bears are not tame, and they are not zoo animals. You have come to their natural habitat in the wild, so steer clear of them as much as possible. Don't try to get closer for a better photo. While deaths from bear attacks have been scant throughout New York's history, hikers in other states and in national parks have been mauled and sustained serious injuries because they tried to get too close—and Randi has had the dubious honor of writing about a lot of them.

- **Carry bear spray.** Pepper spray is one good defense against a charging bear. Nontoxic and with no permanent effect, it triggers "temporary incapacitating discomfort" in the bear, which can halt an attack and give you the opportunity to get away. If a bear charges you, aim the aerosol directly in the bear's face. This is not a bear repellent—spraying it on yourself (as you would an insect repellent) will not keep bears away.

- **If you encounter a bear, do this.** As every bear will react differently, there is no set protocol that will result in a sure-fire escape. Talk quietly or not at all; the time to make loud noise is before you encounter a bear.

  - Try to detour around the bear if possible.

  - Do not run! Talk calmly so that the bear can tell you're human and therefore not a threat—or prey.

  - Make yourself look larger—move to higher ground if you can. Do not climb a tree. Black bears are good climbers and may follow you.

  - Drop something (not food) to distract the bear. Keep your pack on for protection in case of an attack.

  - If a bear attacks and you have pepper spray, use it!

BUGS AND BUTTERFLIES

Mosquitoes, blackflies, no-see-ums, gnats, and other tiny flying things can make a May or June hike less fun than you intended, so take the necessary precautions. Choose an insect repellent that will ward off the bugs you want to avoid, and use it liberally—it's not cologne or aftershave, it's a protective tool; coat your exposed skin with it. We recommend spraying the inside of your hat brim to help keep bugs off your face and ears.

Deer ticks that carry Lyme disease have become a significant issue in New York State. We hiked all the trails in this book without contracting Lyme disease, so the precautions we took seemed to do the job: We treated all our clothing (especially our socks) with insect repellent made for this purpose, wore additional repellent on any exposed skin, and wore long, lightweight pants and boots that covered our ankles. We also checked carefully after hiking to be sure we hadn't taken on any hitchhiking ticks. The few ticks we saw never made it past our clothing. Lyme disease is a serious illness with potential long-term implications—it may seem like overkill to be so cautious, but it will help keep you from getting sick.

On the positive side, you can look forward to seeing lots of butterflies, like eastern tiger swallowtails, black swallowtails, red admirals, monarchs, mourning cloaks, and several others. If you love butterflies, plan a hike through an open meadow or a marsh in spring or

Eastern tiger swallowtails are very common in the Catskills.

summer. Tiny green inchworms may dangle in front of you on a single thread of silk on forest trails, working their way to the ground, where they will pupate below the soil and become geometer moths.

BIRDS

More than 270 bird species either pass through the Catskills during spring and fall migration or nest and breed in the area, so you may spot any number of interesting birds, depending on the season. From spring through fall, virtually all the region's forests host red-eyed vireo, wood thrush, hermit thrush, veery, yellow warbler, common yellowthroat, ovenbird, gray catbird, house wren, white-breasted nuthatch, American robin, blue jay, northern cardinal, northern flicker, downy and hairy woodpeckers, pileated woodpecker, great-crested flycatcher, chipping sparrow, and other common woodland birds.

Red-eyed vireo is one of the most common woodland birds in the Catskills.

A hike that includes open meadows may bring you tree and barn swallows, eastern bluebird, red-winged blackbird, eastern meadowlark, bobolink, and savannah sparrow, as well as northern harrier hunting for small rodents for dinner. Overhead, turkey vultures may circle in their search for carrion; some may glide on the wind at eye level when you reach a mountain summit. Bald eagles are commonly seen dive-fishing along lakes and rivers.

Ospreys nest at the tops of tall poles near lakes and reservoirs.

The ponds and marshy areas are almost sure to attract great blue heron, as well as swamp sparrow, marsh wren, and shorebirds including greater yellowlegs, spotted sandpiper, least and semipalmated sandpipers, and others during their migration. Canada geese are common residents, and wood ducks, blue-winged teal, and green-winged teal spend spring and summer on Catskill ponds. Migration may bring northern pintail, common and red-breasted mergansers, greater and lesser scaups, bufflehead, and ruddy duck. Ospreys are a common sight near lakes, their nests atop utility poles and other very tall structures.

A WORD ABOUT SNAKES

Seventeen snake species occur in New York State, so you may encounter one or two of these as you hike throughout the Catskill region. It's entirely likely that you will spot a completely harmless garter snake or a brown snake on Catskill trails. In some areas, however, it is possible—though uncommon—that you will come across a timber rattlesnake or a copperhead, two of the three venomous snake species that live in this state. (The third, the massasauga rattlesnake, occurs only in two wetlands in central and western New York; it is not found in the Catskills.)

It's unusual—though certainly possible, as Stacey can attest—to encounter a timber rattlesnake in the southeastern portion of New York. Commercial hunters covet their skins, so these snakes have been pursued into threatened status in recent years, making a sighting a fairly rare occurrence on a downstate trail. Watch for a light-colored snake with large dark brown blotches along its 5- to 6-foot length. You may hear the rattle before you see the snake, although other snakes—threatening and benign—vibrate their tails when they are provoked, making a sound like a rattle when the tail encounters dry leaves.

The Catskills are prime territory for the northern copperhead, a light brown snake with distinctive bands around its body that widen along its sides. The copperhead's fairly narrow head has a distinctly coppery hue.

If you encounter a venomous snake on a path, keep your distance and let it pass. In most cases, the snake wants as little to do with you as you do with it and will slither away without bothering you—most snakes don't like to attack something too big to eat. If you get too close unexpectedly and the snake does bite, seek medical attention, including antivenin treatment, immediately. The SUNY College of Environmental Science and Forestry (ESF) recommends that you leave snakebite treatment to medical professionals—the kits that suggest that you cut open the wound with a razor blade and suction out the poison are "not recommended" by the ESF. Adults rarely die of these snakebites, the ESF notes, unless they have a severe allergic reaction to the venom—a very unusual situation.

ABOUT YOUR DOG

You can bring your dog along on just about every hike in this book, but that does not necessarily mean you should. Hikes that require scrambling or rock climbing may be too difficult or complex for a dog to negotiate, leaving you to carry your pet up tricky stretches—just when you really need both hands to be safe.

With the abundant wildlife in the Catskills, encounters between dogs and coyotes, foxes, beavers, snakes, or bears can result in confrontations, any of which can end badly for your dog.

We have endeavored to provide information in each hike description to help you decide if the hike you have chosen is truly dog-friendly or if your pup should sit this one out. In general, however, flat or hilly hikes in fairly open country will be safer for your dog than treks over very rocky terrain with substantial elevation gains.

PANDEMIC ETIQUETTE

As we write this, the COVID-19 pandemic dominates news headlines and continues to spread through most of the United States. The Centers for Disease Control and Prevention (CDC) has said that it is safe to be outdoors without masks if we practice social distancing, but we still encounter people on the trail who are not vaccinated—especially children under 12 years old. This gives us an opportunity to establish some trail etiquette for our time.

- If a hiking party is approaching in front of you, step aside to let them pass, and maintain at least 6 feet of distance between you.

- If there are small children with the party, carry a mask that you can put on quickly as they approach.

- Carry hand sanitizer to use after you touch railings, fences, benches, or other objects that are used frequently by hikers.

As we have all learned since early 2020, being outdoors provides one of the best ways to cope with the restrictions of pandemic life. A few simple precautions help us enjoy our time in the wilderness while protecting ourselves from the virus.

WILDERNESS REGULATIONS

Most of the hikes in this book cross New York state parks or lands protected as part of the New York Forest Preserve by the Department of Environmental Conservation. Other land protection agencies represented in this book include local city and county park commissions, The Nature Conservancy, land trust organizations, and private foundations or associations.

While regulations may differ from one organization to the next—especially where dogs are concerned—they agree on these commonsense rules:

- **Stay within the park boundaries.** Adjacent lands may be privately owned; please be considerate of others' property.

- **Keep dogs leashed, and pick up their waste.** Some properties do not allow dogs; check the listings in this book before you hike.

- **Do not pick flowers, remove plants, or destroy plants or trees.** The adage "Take only memories, leave only footprints" is in effect here.

- **Leave artifacts in place as you found them.** Moving or removing an artifact can diminish its value in revealing facts about the area's history and is illegal in many areas.

- **Carry out all your trash.** This is a rule that many Catskills hikers neglect to follow, so you will see trash—sometimes piles of it—in some of the most popular areas. Don't consider this permission to leave your own cans and wrappers. Please take your own trash out of the park.

- **Tagging is against the law.** Some popular trails have become targets for graffiti artists, especially those closer to New York City. Tagging is a Class A misdemeanor in New York State, punishable with fines and up to a year in prison. Resist the urge to follow the example of inconsiderate people who don't understand the value of pristine wilderness.

As cute as chipmunks are, they should not eat food made for humans.

- **Stay on marked trails.** Using "social trails," like shortcuts across switchbacks, causes hillsides to erode more quickly, which will eventually destroy the landscape. Stick to the nicely cleared, engineered, and maintained trails.
- **Don't feed the animals.** Chipmunks, squirrels, deer, geese, ducks, and other creatures will not benefit from becoming accustomed to handouts from humans. Feeding them can actually make them dangerous, as they begin to approach humans for food and may become aggressive. This is especially true of bears, which have the ability to overpower a person.

YOUR SAFETY: THE TEN ESSENTIALS

Any time you step out on a trail, you may encounter situations that require an abrupt change of plans. Maybe you miss a turn and find yourself lost in the wilderness. Perhaps a storm front moves in without warning, or someone in your party sustains an injury. Any of these circumstances can extend your time outdoors, turning a day hike into an overnight stay or forcing you to seek cover off-trail.

You're not the first to feel compromised in the backcountry—in fact, it happens often enough that there's a checklist of things you should have with you every time you hike. The list is known as the Ten Essentials, items that can help you take control of your situation and make it back home in one piece. It was first developed by the Mountaineers, a club for hikers and climbers, back in the 1930s; they've since updated it in their book *Mountaineering: The Freedom of the Hills*, in which they group some individual items to provide a more thorough list.

If you carry all these things with you on every hike, you'll be ready no matter what nature throws at you.

1. Navigation tools: a good map and compass
2. Sun protection: sunscreen and sunglasses
3. Insulation: extra clothing and a poncho
4. Illumination: flashlight and/or headlamp
5. First-aid kit
6. Fire starter: lighter and/or waterproof matches
7. Repair kit and tools
8. Nutrition: more food than you think you will need
9. Hydration: more water than you think you will need
10. Emergency shelter: emergency space blanket or ultralight tarp

Keep in mind that while your smartphone may provide maps and a bright light, it will run out of power in the great outdoors and you'll have nowhere to charge it. Equally important, there's no cellular service on most of these hikes, especially those in state parks or on trails that lead to mountain summits. If you're going to bring a GPS device with you, choose one that relies on satellites, not on cellular—and bring extra batteries.

HIKES	BEST HIKES FOR WATERFALLS	BEST HIKES FOR SUMMITS	BEST HIKES FOR VIEWS	BEST HIKES FOR HISTORY	BEST HIKES FOR SCRAMBLES	BEST KID-FRIENDLY HIKES
1. Burnt Knob-Acra Point			•			
2. Colgate Lake to Dutcher Notch						•
3. Mountain Top Arboretum						•
4. North-South Lake Park: Catskill Escarpment Loop	•		•			•
5. Kaaterskill and Bastion Falls	•					
6. West Kill Mountain	•		•		•	
7. Dibble's Quarry			•	•		•
8. Huckleberry Point Trail	•		•			•
9. Plattekill Preserve Falls	•		•			•
10. Codfish Point	•		•			
11. Echo Lake	•		•			
12. Overlook Mountain			•			
13. Opus 40				•		
14. Bluestone Wild Forest: Onteora Lake			•			•
15. Ashokan Reservoir Promenade and Rail Trail			•	•		•
16. Ashokan Quarry Trail			•	•		•
17. Ashokan High Point					•	
18. Wallkill Valley Rail Trail: New Paltz to Rosendale			•			•

#	Trail	Col 1	Col 2	Col 3	Col 4	Col 5	Col 6
21.	Pratt Rock Trail	●		●			
22.	Rochester Hollow	●		●			
23.	Giant Ledge/Panther Mountain		●		●	●	
24.	Slide Mountain				●	●	
25.	Table Mountain		●		●	●	
26.	Red Hill Fire Tower			●	●		
27.	Willowemoc Wild Forest: Frick Pond Trail	●			●		
28.	Shaupeneak Ridge Park				●		●
29.	John Burroughs Nature Sanctuary	●		●	●		●
30.	Bonticou Crag		●		●		
31.	Millbrook Ridge	●	●		●		
32.	Gertrude's Nose/Minnewaska Trail	●			●		
33.	Undercliff/Overcliff Trail	●					
34.	Minnewaska Lake Carriage Road	●			●		
35.	Minnewaska SPP: Rainbow Falls Trail	●					●
36.	Minnewaska SPP: Stony Kill Falls	●					●
37.	Shawangunk Grasslands NWR	●			●		
38.	Minnewaska SPP: Sam's Point Road to the Ice Caves	●			●		
39.	Upper Falls of Vernooy Kill	●					●
40.	Delaware and Hudson Canal Linear Park	●		●			
41.	Bethel Woods Bindy Bazaar	●		●			
42.	Minisink Battleground Park	●		●			

MAP LEGEND

Transportation

Symbol	Name
84	Interstate Highway
6	US Highway
28	State Highway
110	County/Forest Road
= = = =	Unpaved Road
------	Featured Trail
------	Trail or Fire Road

Water Features

- Body of Water
- River/Creek
- Waterfall
- Spring

Symbols

- ① Trailhead
- ▲ Mountain/Peak
- 🅿 Parking
- Scenic Overview
- ▪ Point of Interest
- Tower
- Bridge
- Picnic Area
- Bench

Land Management

- Wilderness Area
- State/Local Park

NORTHEASTERN CATSKILLS

Here's where you'll find some of the most popular and most spectacular hikes in the Catskills. Miles of trails lead to views that are phenomenal in every season. Kaaterskill Falls is here—arguably the park's crown jewel, featuring New York State's highest cascading waterfall. There's a reason nearby trails include Inspiration Point, Artist's Rock, and Poet's Ledge.

Some of the Catskills' highest peaks offer challenging hiking in this part of the park, such as Sugarloaf, Blackhead, West Kill, and Kaaterskill High Peak.

Fish, swim, or paddle in Colgate Lake or North–South Lake (where there's a public campground). Mountain bike on more than 120 miles of trails.

Covering Greene and Ulster Counties, this section of Catskill Park is called the Catskill Escarpment. The mountains here were created by glaciers, which eroded their tops. From a distance they seem smooth and rounded, but don't let that fool you: There are plenty of crags, boulders, and rock walls to challenge you.

Still, numerous easy and moderate hikes help balance out a weekend, like Dibble's Quarry and Huckleberry Point Trail. In recent years, the Ashokan Reservoir has brought visitors to its beautiful, accessible promenade walk and nearby rail trail.

You'll come across the names (and paths) of several long trails time and again—in particular, the Finger Lakes Trail (FLT) and the Long Path. These trails traverse the mountains, running along their spines and branching out to myriad individual trails.

The FLT, whose general direction is east–west, is the longest continuous hiking trail in New York State. It begins on the New York–Pennsylvania border in Allegheny State Park and runs 549 miles to the junction of the Long Path in the Catskills.

The Long Path is a north–south trail. It begins in New York City at the foot of the George Washington Bridge and runs nearly 350 miles north, where it passes through (sometimes on roads) many counties, preserves, state parks, and forests before entering the Catskill Forest Preserve—where it continues for more than 90 miles and crosses eleven high peaks over 3,500 feet. It ends at John Boyd Thacher State Park, about 15 miles southwest of Albany, New York.

Then there's the Devil's Path, which runs for 24 miles, east–west across six mountains: Indian Head, Twin, Sugarloaf, and Plateau—which define the Indian Head Wilderness area—Hunter, and West Kill. With 7,800 feet of elevation gain, rock scrambles, and cliff bands, it's got the reputation as the toughest hike in the Catskills.

The New York–New Jersey Trail Conference, the New York State Department of Environmental Conservation, and other organizations such as the Catskill Center for Conservation and Development, the Catskill Mountain Club, the Catskill 3500 Club, the New York City Department of Environmental Protection, the Open Space Institute, and many local organizations do an amazing job of maintaining these trails.

Since the Catskills are so close to New York City, the trails on this side of the park have been popular since the late 1800s and remain so today. They are heavily traveled, particularly on weekends.

In addition, the COVID-19 pandemic brought an unusually high number of hikers to the area. The Catskill Center reported that in 2020, park stewards at three high-use areas of the park—Kaaterskill Falls, Peekamoose Blue Hole, and Platte Clove—greeted 70,000 visitors, a 27 percent increase from the previous year. As you create an itinerary, try to arrange weekday hiking, if possible. And get to trailheads early to find parking.

View from Sam's Point

1 BURNT KNOB–ACRA POINT

A relatively easy way to check out two viewpoints along the Escarpment Trail and enjoy a panorama of Blackhead and Black Dome.

County: Greene
Start: Big Hollow Road (NY 56) parking lot
Elevation gain: 1,030 feet
Distance: 6.5-mile round-trip
Difficulty: Moderate
Hiking time: About 3.25 hours
Seasons: Year-round
Schedule: Open daily; camping areas available
Fees and permits: No fees or permits required
Trail contact: DEC Region 4 Stamford Office (Mon through Fri, 8:30 a.m. to 4:30 p.m.); (607) 652-7365; email: r4.ump@dec.ny.gov
Canine compatibility: Dogs permitted on leash

Trail surface: Roots, rocks, streambeds
Land status: New York State Department of Environmental Conservation
Nearest town: Windham, New York
Other trail users: Snowshoers (in season)
Maps: CalTopo Burnt Knob Catskills (caltopo.com/m/QAHA); New York–New Jersey Trail Conference Trail Map 141
Special considerations: The last mile of the road to the trailhead is considered seasonal and is not maintained during the winter. If there's heavy snowfall, you may park on the side of the road. The parking area is rarely plowed.

FINDING THE TRAILHEAD

From the New York State Thruway, take exit 20 (Saugerties). Turn left on NY 212/NY 32. At the traffic light turn right on NY 32 North. Drive 6 miles and continue straight on NY 32A. Drive 1.9 miles; turn left on NY 23A. Head up the winding road toward Tannersville. Drive through town and turn right at the traffic light onto Hill Street (CR 23C). Stay on that for 6.1 miles. Turn right on CR 40. In about 2 miles you'll come to the hamlet of Maplecrest. Veer right onto Big Hollow Road (NY 56) and drive 4 miles. The parking lot, which is at the end of the road, is about 0.2 mile past the trailhead. Trailhead GPS: N42 17.360' / W74 06.963'

THE HIKE

If you're a Rip Van Winkle fan, you've come to the right place. Burnt Knob and Acra Point are two spots on the Escarpment Trail on a lower peak in the Windham-Blackhead Wilderness, RVW's sleeping and stomping grounds. The trail and the views it offers were also the inspiration for nineteenth-century Hudson River School painters such as Thomas Cole and Frederic Church.

The Escarpment Trail, which is part of the nearly 350-mile Long Path, runs for just under 24 miles end to end and makes a great long-weekend camping and hiking trip. (Just remember to leave a vehicle at each end.) Note that there are no official, designated campsites in the Burnt Knob–Acra Point col (a saddle between two peaks).

But if you've only got a few hours, hiking to Acra Point and Burnt Knob (named for the forest fires that have destroyed hundreds of acres of the Catskills over the centuries) at least gives you a sense of this beautiful trail that wanders across creeks, through dense

Elves and fairies would appreciate the picturesque path leading through the forest.

hardwood forest filled with hemlock and spruce trees, and offers stunning views. As you walk the picturesque the trail, you half expect elves and fairies to dart out.

Finding the trailhead may be a bit challenging, but there are signs. From the parking lot, go down the gravel road to the trail entrance on the right. You start out on the Black Dome Trail and right away cross the Batavia Kill on a wooden footbridge. You'll cross more water soon, and if there's been a lot of rain or snowmelt, you may not be able to cross without getting wet. Then there's a relatively steady but not too arduous uphill climb over roots and rocks for about 1.0 mile until you come to the junction with the Escarpment Trail and choose your destination. Either way leads to a great view.

MILES AND DIRECTIONS

0.0   Start at the trailhead, pick up the Black Dome Trail, and follow the red markers into the woods. You'll soon cross a small wooden bridge over Batavia Kill. Sign in at the register on the other side of the bridge. There will be more water to cross soon and no footbridge. For the next 0.5 mile you'll follow the creek as you walk uphill.

1.1   T junction with the Escarpment Trail. Choose to go to Acra Point (to the right) or Burnt Knob (to the left). We turned left to Burnt Knob, following the blue-blazed trail.

1.4   Social trail on your left offers an outstanding view of Windham High Peak.

2.6   You've reached the large rock that is the "burnt knob." The view is best when the leaves are down. From here you can see Acra Point. Turn and head back to the main trail.

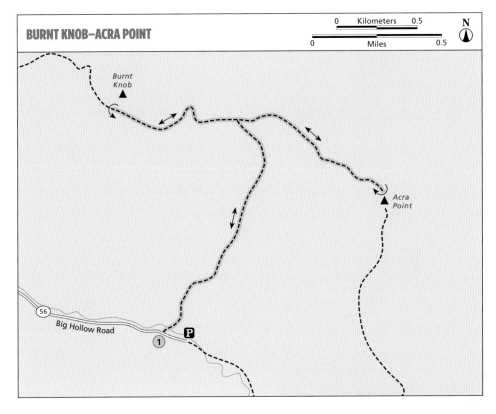

0   Kilometers   0.5

0   Miles   0.5

N

Burnt
Knob

Acra
Point

56

Big Hollow Road

P

1

4.1 Back at the junction, turn right and return to the parking area, or stay on the blue-blazed trail to Acra Point. The trail becomes steeper, and there are a few boulders to climb over along the way.

4.2 Social trail to left with viewpoint. Nothing to see if there are leaves on the trees. Stay straight, following the blue markers. In a few feet, look to your right; you'll see a yellow marker. Follow this little yellow-blazed trail for maybe 30 to 40 feet and you'll get rewarded with a great view of large mountains that feel really close. Turn around and head back onto the blue-blazed trail for about another 0.5 mile through the woods.

4.7 You've reached Acra Point and a large flat rock. You can also see Burnt Knob from here. It's a great place for lunch and to view the Blackhead Range. Turn around and return to the trailhead the way you came.

6.5 Arrive back at the trailhead.

The well-marked trail offers great options to continue your hiking.

2 COLGATE LAKE TO DUTCHER NOTCH

Double the fun: a beautiful spot for a picnic and swim with a nearby easy hiking trail—a real walk in the woods—and spots for camping.

County: Greene
Start: Colgate Lake Trail parking, Colgate Road
Elevation gain: 385 feet
Distance: 9.2 miles out and back
Difficulty: Easy
Hiking time: About 4 hours
Seasons: Year-round
Schedule: Open daily; camping areas available
Fees and permits: No fees or permits required
Trail contact: DEC Region 4 Stamford Office (Mon through Fri, 8:30 a.m. to 4:30 p.m.); (607) 652-7365; email: r4.ump@dec.ny.gov

Canine compatibility: Dogs permitted on leash
Trail surface: Soil, boggy areas
Land status: New York State Department of Environmental Conservation
Nearest town: Tannersville, New York
Other trail users: Cross-country skiers, snowshoers (in season)
Maps: AllTrails Dutcher Notch (alltrails.com/explore/recording/dutcher-notch-0f20c77); New York–New Jersey Trail Conference Trail Map 141
Special considerations: This trail can be very muddy after a heavy rain or snowmelt.

FINDING THE TRAILHEAD

Take the New York State Thruway to exit 21 (Catskill). Take a left out of the NYS Thruway entrance road and go approximately 0.25 mile. Take a right onto NY 23 West and go approximately 6.6 miles to Cairo, New York. Turn left onto NY 32 (there's a McDonald's Restaurant on the corner) and travel approximately 7.7 miles. Turn right onto NY 23A and go approximately 9 miles to Tannersville (6.9 miles if you come from Saugerties via Palenville). Turn right at the traffic light in Tannersville onto CR 23C and continue approximately 3 miles to Jewett. Turn right onto CR 78 to Colgate Lake and go approximately 1.7 miles, *past* Colgate Lake. There are two DEC parking lots on the left side of the road. You want the *second* lot off the dirt road. Trailhead GPS: N42 14.330' / W74 06.981'

THE HIKE

Located in the 1,500-acre Colgate Lake Wild Forest, the Colgate Lake Trail connects with the Escarpment Trail, which runs for just under 24 miles end to end and is part of the 347-mile Long Path. Part of what makes the Colgate Trail unique is that it's a very easy hike in what is normally rugged terrain.

This is a hike to savor. Go all the way to Dutcher Notch, or just hike for a mile or 2 and turn back. If you've been doing some hard hiking, this is a time to let your beat feet meander along wide, soft paths.

Being the Catskills, of course, there are views, but they actually come at the hike's beginning, since the forest is surrounded by the Windham-Blackhead Range Wilderness on three sides. As you walk across the field to the woods, you'll be able to see Blackhead and Arizona Mountains.

The views come at the start of your hike; the forest is surrounded by the Windham-Blackhead Range Wilderness on three sides.

It's a pretty walk over wooden bridges that cross creeks and bogs—and no elevation to speak of. You'll wander through an old apple orchard, and, if you're quiet enough, you can hear the sound of a 15-foot waterfall just off the path.

Once you reach Dutcher Notch, there's a four-way intersection and a trail sign for Arizona and Blackhead Mountains (left) and Stoppel Point and North Mountain (right). Time to choose to hike more or return to the parking area. From there, why not go

Colgate Lake, across the road from the hiking trails, is a great spot to swim, paddle, or fish. A creek runs below the dam.

across the street to Colgate Lake? You can move your vehicle to the other, lake parking lot. Campsites and other trails hide in the woods behind this parking area.

At the lake, you can camp, use small boats, fish, or swim. A short hike winds partially around the lake, but if the water level is too high, the path will be covered.

MILES AND DIRECTIONS

0.0 Start at the Colgate Lake parking area. You'll see a gate near the lot, where the trail begins. Don't let it fool you. There's a yellow marker at the entrance to the trail-head, which is to the right of the gate. Depending on the season, the trail may be overgrown. But hike across the field until you get to the woods, where you will see another yellow marker.

1.1 Sign in at the register and turn left on the yellow-blazed trail. There might be a tepee made of sticks left by previous hikers to make sure you don't miss the turn and the trail marker. Very gradual climb.

1.2 Cross the wooden bridge (#1) over the creek and follow the yellow markers. Go up a small hill to a well-marked crossroads; turn left. (Going to the right might possibly take you to private land.)

1.5 Pay attention as the trail bears right to follow the yellow markers. Stay the course, and don't wander off onto the social trails and logging roads along the way. They lead to private land.

2.0 Bear left and continue following the yellow markers. You'll cross a creek over a small wooden bridge (#2) then walk through some overgrown vegetation for about 30 yards. The area turns marshy, and you'll soon cross another bridge. Continue following the yellow trail markers.

COLGATE LAKE TO DUTCHER NOTCH

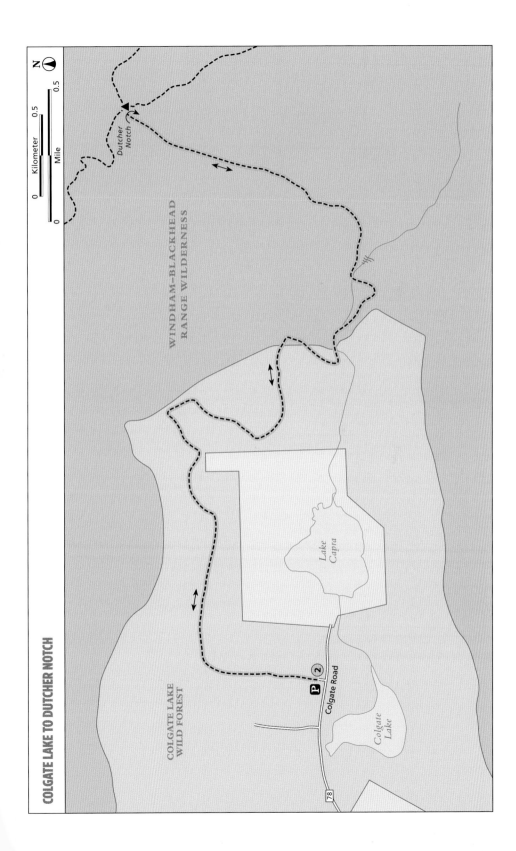

A wooden walkway helps hikers traverse the boggy, marshy path.

2.3 Cross bridge number three.

3.1 Cross bridge number four.

3.3 Waterfall about 150 feet off the trail.

4.6 Reach Dutcher Notch. Retrace your steps to the parking lot.

9.2 Arrive back at the parking lot.

3 MOUNTAIN TOP ARBORETUM

A chance to wind down in a contemplative public garden featuring native trees, plants, and birds.

County: Greene
Start: Mountain Top Arboretum, 4 Maude Adams Rd., Tannersville
Elevation gain: 314 feet
Distance: 2.7 miles of trails
Difficulty: Easy
Hiking time: 1–2 hours
Seasons: Year-round
Schedule: Open daily, dawn to dusk. The education center is open 9 a.m. to 4 p.m., Tues through Sat.
Fees and permits: No fees or permits required; donations encouraged
Trail contact: Mountain Top Arboretum, 4 Maude Adams Rd., Tannersville 12485; (518) 589-3903; email: info@arboretum.org

Canine compatibility: Dogs permitted on leash on Maude Adams Road and the East Meadow; off leash on Spruce Glen trails. Dogs are not permitted in the West Meadow or the Woodland Walk.
Trail surface: Soft surfaces—grass, mulch, gravel, soil
Land status: The arboretum is a 501c3 nonprofit organization.
Nearest town: Tannersville, New York
Other trail users: Dog walkers
Maps: Mountain Top Arboretum self-guided tours (mtarboretum.org/self-guided-tours)
Special considerations: Although it is mostly flat, the soft terrain may make it difficult to push a stroller or propel a wheelchair.

FINDING THE TRAILHEAD

Take the New York State Thruway to exit 20 (Saugerties). Turn left at the traffic light for 0.1 mile, then turn right on NY 32. After 6 miles, take the left fork onto NY 32A to Palenville. At the traffic light, turn left onto NY 23A. Continue west to Tannersville, then turn right at the traffic light onto CR 23C. After 2 miles, turn right onto the dirt road, Maude Adams Road, and continue 50 yards to the arboretum parking area. Trailhead GPS: N42 22.215' / W74 13.476'

THE HIKE

The Mountain Top Arboretum was founded by Peter and Bonnie Ahrens, whose summer home overlooked a 7-acre parcel of mountaintop scrubland. The couple turned those acres into a public garden in 1977. Since then, the arboretum has grown to 178 acres. The arboretum is committed to land stewardship and holds public lectures and programs related to the environment and the importance of the Catskill Mountains.

If you've ever wondered about the emerald ash borer or about the very bedrock you walk on in the Catskills, the arboretum is the place for you. Plant collections, meadows, wetlands, and forest crisscross the arboretum. Search for birds, and visit the educational center with guest speakers and programs for people of all ages.

The site is divided into four sections—West and East Meadows, Woodland Walk, and Spruce Glen. The West Meadow features a rain garden and spiral labyrinth as well as plants that can weather the Catskills' sometimes harsh conditions: bedrock, thin soil, wind, and exposure. The exposed bedrock in this section dates to the Devonian period and is about 375 million years old.

Pink mountain laurel Carol hugs the pond in the arboretum's West Meadow. A stand of dawn redwood makes a fine backdrop. STACEY FREED

The Woodland Walk is set behind a deer-exclusion gate. Here the arboretum studies, preserves, and displays native habitats of the northern Catskills. Three connected paths take you through areas of native wildflowers and mountain laurel, an amphitheater, and a fairy garden.

In the East Meadow are a long allée of white pines, a pumphouse that helps irrigate the plantings, and a wet-meadow boardwalk. Looking across the meadow you'll see the mountains around Platte Clove.

Just past the East Meadow, Spruce Glen comprises three ecosystems created by changes in elevation and moisture level. The glen holds a hidden marsh and wetlands, a spruce nursery, old-growth hemlock, and fir, birch, beech, and maple trees.

MILES AND DIRECTIONS

From the parking lot head left to the gate to enter the designated walk through the arboretum. Choose any of the four areas to begin your walk. We went this way:

0.0 Parking area off CR 23C and Maude Adams Road. Walk a few hundred feet to the Woodland Walk on the right. Follow the three looping trails around the wildflowers and mountain laurel, outdoor classroom, and fairy garden. This area encompasses about 0.2 mile.

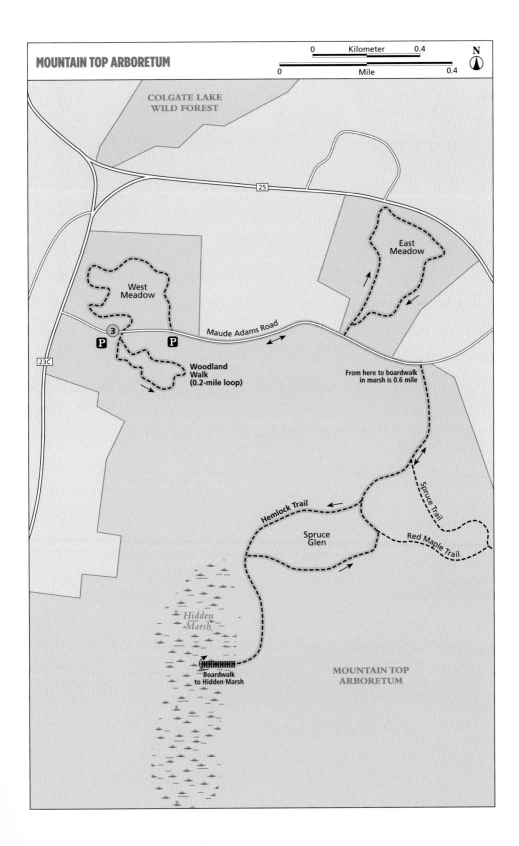

MOUNTAIN TOP ARBORETUM

0   Kilometer   0.4

0   Mile   0.4

N

COLGATE LAKE
WILD FOREST

25

East
Meadow

West
Meadow

23C

Maude Adams Road

P   P

Woodland
Walk
(0.2-mile loop)

From here to boardwalk
in marsh is 0.6 mile

Spruce Trail

Hemlock Trail

Spruce
Glen

Red Maple Trail

Hidden
Marsh

Boardwalk
to Hidden Marsh

MOUNTAIN TOP
ARBORETUM

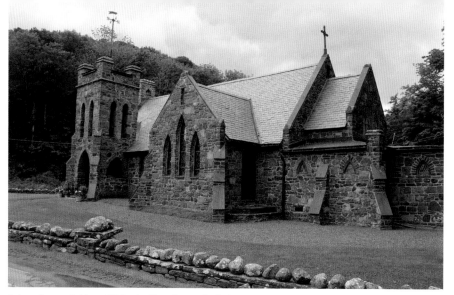

Arboretum neighbor, All Souls Church, was built in 1894 in the Gothic Revival style. It's on the National Register of Historic Places.

0.2 Cross the road and visit the West Meadow. There is no path so to speak, but wander through areas marked Rain Garden, Bird Cove, Spiral Labyrinth, Dwarf Conifers, and Dawn Redwoods and Bedrock. From here, turn left on Maude Adams Road (a dirt road; no cars are allowed on this road).

0.6 Turn left into East Meadow. Bear right to cross the boardwalk. Turn left at the junction with the pumphouse and continue to loop around, heading left. You'll pass the hedge row and pine allée and make your way back to Maude Adams Road.

1.0 Turn left on Maude Adams Road, then turn right onto the Hemlock Trail.

1.6 Hidden Marsh wetlands. Head back the way you came.

1.8 Turn right onto Hemlock Ridge.

2.0 Bear right on Red Maple Trail.

2.2 Turn left on Spruce Trail.

2.4 Turn right onto Hemlock Trail to head back to the parking lot.

2.7 Arrive back at the parking lot.

Summertime blooms at the Mountain Top Arboretum.

4 NORTH–SOUTH LAKE PARK: CATSKILL ESCARPMENT LOOP

There's no better way to take in the vibrant Catskill Mountains scenery than on this trail, where you will see the area from many angles.

County: Greene
Start: Parking area on Scutt Road just before entrance to North–South Lake Campground
Elevation gain: 509 feet
Distance: 4.9-mile lollipop
Difficulty: Strenuous
Hiking time: About 4 hours
Seasons: Spring through fall
Schedule: Trail open 24/7
Fees and permits: Day-use fee at entrance for parking during peak seasons; no fee to hike this trail
Trail contact: North–South Lake Campground, CR 18, Haines Falls 12436; (518) 357-2289 or (518) 589-5058; dec.ny.gov/outdoor/24487.html
Canine compatibility: Dogs permitted on leash. (You may be asked to provide proof of a valid rabies inoculation at the campground entrance.)

Trail surface: Dirt and rock, some scrambling up large rocks
Land status: New York State Department of Environmental Conservation
Nearest town: Haines Falls, New York
Other trail users: Mountain bikers; equestrians on yellow-blazed sections
Maps: NatGeo TOPO! Map (USGS) Kaaterskill Clove; NatGeo Trails Illustrated Map #755: Catskill Park; trail map available online at catskillmountaineer.com/hiking-escarpment-SW.html
Special considerations: Black bears live in the Catskills, and they are frequently spotted in the vicinity of this trail. Before you undertake this hike, make sure you know what to do if you come across a bear in the woods. (See "Critters" in this book's introduction.)

FINDING THE TRAILHEAD

From the south, take I-87 North to exit 20 at Saugerties. Follow NY 32 North for approximately 6 miles to NY 32A to NY 23A West. Stay on NY 23A to the village of Haines Falls. Take your first right onto CR 18. The campground entrance is at the end of the road in 2 miles.

From the north, take I-87 South to exit 21 at Catskill. Turn left onto NY 23 East and continue to US 9W South. Follow US 9W through Catskill to NY 23A. Follow 23A West to Haines Falls. Make the first right turn in Haines Falls onto CR 18. The campground entrance is at the end of the road in 2 miles. Trailhead GPS: N42 12.045' / W74 03.511'

THE HIKE

If you've wondered about the best places to see the most sweeping views of the Catskill Mountains in their full glory—especially in fall—this solid hiking experience is for you. Make a day of it, and explore all the side trails that lead to slices of the region's history in hospitality and tourism, and from which you can see the views that inspired the first truly American style and philosophy of fine art: the Hudson River School of landscape painting.

Three major resorts served guests during the "season" here from the mid-1800s into the mid-1900s: Kaaterskill Hotel, Laurel House, and the venerable Catskill Mountain

Take the bridge to see Kaaterskill Falls from the top.

House. These hotels drew the wealthiest city dwellers from all over the state and beyond, including a core group of artists of a uniquely American approach to painting known as the Hudson River School. Artists, including Thomas Cole, came to the Catskill Mountain House to paint the extraordinary view from its front lawn—Cole's famous *A View of the Two Lakes and Mountain House, Catskill Mountains, Morning* was one result. Authors Washington Irving, James Fenimore Cooper, and John Bartram all referred to this resort in their writings, and three US presidents—Ulysses Grant, Chester Arthur, and Theodore Roosevelt—came here for a respite from the pressures of the office.

Your hike begins in the parking area at North–South Lake Campground, a stunningly beautiful area in its own right. From the Scutt Road parking area, walk up Scutt Road (it's easier and less annoying than the root-crossed blue-blazed trail at this point, though they both lead to the main trailhead) and then follow the trail marked with blue DEC markers. Stay on the blue-blazed trail for most of this hike, leaving it to enhance your experience with side trails to magnificent Kaaterskill Falls, one of New York State's most dramatic waterfalls, and to the sites of the former Kaaterskill Hotel and Catskill Mountain House, two of the most popular mountain retreats for the wealthy when the Catskills provided a respite from the intense heat and foul air of a New York City summer.

Many of the landmarks that once dotted this land now remain only as foundations and memories, so Layman's Monument stands out as a place where you may want to linger. This stone obelisk commemorates the courage of 25-year-old firefighter Frank Layman, who died here on August 10, 1900, when a forest fire engulfed him before he could jump off the ledge to escape. The monument stands where his comrades found him once the fire was under control, making this a particularly poignant place to pause as you walk this trail through the landscape he gave his life to save.

After Layman's Monument, scramble up to a series of narrow ledges that provide stunning views of the mountains, distant ravines and waterfalls, and valleys that make the Catskills such a popular place to hike. Watch your step as you traverse these slender overlooks; if you want to enjoy the view before you continue, stop walking while you do so.

When you're not faced with one wide, entrancing view of the area after another, your hike takes you through forested lands dominated by red maple, beech, and oak trees, with some stands of paper birch and a scattering of hemlocks. The fragrant woods attract a wide variety of birds and small furry animals, as well as white-tailed deer and the occasional black bear. Keep your eyes and ears open for species you may not normally see in your own backyard, including deer, porcupine, and fisher, a weasel-like animal reintroduced in the Catskills in the early 1900s after hunters and trappers had extirpated them. Some lucky hikers have the chance to spot a bobcat, an animal of minimal danger to humans.

Kaaterskill Falls drops 264 feet from this point—and this is just the top half of the falls.

After some scrambling and lots of uphill, the view makes it all worthwhile.

MILES AND DIRECTIONS

0.0   Start from the Scutt Road parking area and walk south on Scutt Road.

0.4   Turn left and walk past the barrier.

0.5   At the trailhead, turn right, following the trail with blue trail markers. Immediately cross a bridge over a creek.

0.6   Stop and register at the registry box. In a few minutes you will reach a major trail junction; go right on the Escarpment Trail (blue markers). If you want to explore a side trail right away, follow the signs across a bridge to your right. This takes you to a viewpoint for the top portion of magnificent Kaaterskill Falls, one of the tallest and most photographed falls in New York State. This side trail adds only about 0.4 mile to your overall hike.

1.2   Reach Layman's Monument. The trail turns left (east) here; continue to follow it. This part of the trail can be very wet in spring and early summer, or after a hard rain.

1.3   Just after a scramble up some large rocks, reach the first of several ledges (overlooks). This one provides a great view of Santa Cruz Falls and Buttermilk Ravine, where you may glimpse Buttermilk Falls.

1.4   This overlook provides more views of Buttermilk Falls and Buttermilk Ravine.

1.6   The yellow- and blue-blazed trails cross here. Continue straight on the Escarpment (blue-blazed) Trail. (The yellow-blazed trail goes back to Scutt Road.)

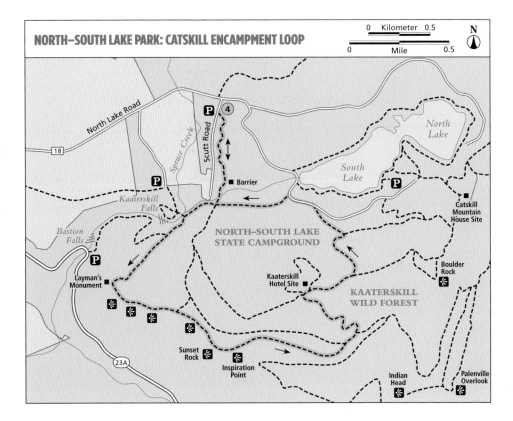

NORTH–SOUTH LAKE PARK: CATSKILL ENCAMPMENT LOOP

1.7 At Sunset Ledge, you can look west toward Haines Falls and enjoy an iconic view of the Catskills.

1.8 Inspiration Point offers an exceptional view of the edge of the Catskills and the valley beyond.

2.0 This overlook affords views of Poet's Ledge, Viola Ravine and Falls, Wildcat Ravine, Indian Head Ledge, and Buttermilk Ravine. The peaks in front of you are Kaaterskill High Peak and Round Top Mountain.

2.6 At the trail junction turn right on the Escarpment Trail. (The other trail will take you back to the parking area.) In less than 0.1 mile, another trail junction offers a route to Palenville Overlook and Palenville; bear left to stay on the Escarpment Trail loop.

3.0 At the junction with the trail to the Kaaterskill Hotel site, go straight for the short loop around the former hotel site or turn right on the Escarpment Trail.

3.3 Come to the junction with the trail to North–South Lake. Turn left to go to the lake, or keep going straight to visit Boulder Rock and the Catskill Mountain House site. This adds about 1.0 mile to your total hike but features some terrific views. When you're ready, continue left on this trail to North–South Lake. Watch your step on the Horseshoe Corner.

3.8 Reach North Lake Road and turn left on the road.

3.9 At the cross-country ski trail, turn left (off the road). Rejoin the main trail.

4.3 You're back at the beginning of the main trail. Turn right to return to your vehicle.

4.9 Arrive back at the parking area.

5 KAATERSKILL AND BASTION FALLS

The tallest waterfall in New York State serves as one of the Catskills' most iconic sights.

County: Greene
Start: Parking area for Kaaterskill Clove on NY 23A
Elevation gain: 330 feet to the base of the falls; an additional 264 feet to the top
Distance: 2.2 miles out and back, including stairs to top of the falls
Difficulty: Moderate
Hiking time: About 1.5 hours
Seasons: Spring through fall
Schedule: Open daily, dawn to dusk
Fees and permits: None
Trail contact: New York State Department of Environmental Conservation (NYSDEC) Division of Lands & Forests, 625 Broadway, 5th Floor, Albany 12233; (518) 473-9518; dec.ny.gov/lands/80993.html
Canine compatibility: Dogs permitted on leash
Trail surface: Dirt path, rock steps/ledges, long staircase

Land status: Public land, managed by NYSDEC
Nearest town: Catskill, New York
Other trail users: Generally just hikers
Maps: Catskill Mountaineer Kaaterskill Falls (catskillmountaineer.com/NSL-KF.html)
Special considerations: The small parking area fills up early on nice days and remains full throughout the day. If you park along the side of NY 23A, pull your car completely off the road. There may be dozens of cars parked along this high-speed road, so take precautions to avoid accidents. This trail can be dangerous in wet or icy conditions; hiking in winter is not recommended. Stay on the trail; do not attempt to stand in the swiftly flowing river at the top of the falls or at the midpoint shelf.

FINDING THE TRAILHEAD

From the town of Catskill, take NY 23A West for 13.2 miles to the bend in the road at Bastion Falls. Pass the falls and turn into the parking area on the left side of the road, about 0.2 mile after the falls. Trailhead GPS: N42 11.387' / W74 04.456'

THE HIKE

If you only have time to take one hike in the Catskill Mountains, make it this one—a challenging 0.5 mile up a narrow, rocky path to one of the finest sights in the entire region. Kaaterskill Falls boasts a higher height than any of Niagara's three falls, and its towering geological setting provides the payoff for the half hour of scrambling you will do to get up here.

Does this waterfall look familiar, even though you've never been here? Perhaps you're a fan of the Hudson River School of American artists, many of whom painted iconic landscapes featuring Kaaterskill Falls. As far back as 1825, artist Thomas Cole discovered the charms of this wilderness after reading about it in Washington Irving's famous short story "Rip Van Winkle." His remarkable painting of the falls became a cover of the *New York Evening Post*, attracting many other artists to settle in nearby Palenville and paint Kaaterskill Falls and other gorgeous sights in the Catskill region. These paintings inspired

Kaaterskill Falls inspired the artists of the Hudson River School.

tourists to travel here to see the falls and the Catskill Mountains for themselves, launching more than a century and a half of intensive tourist activity in this remote part of New York State.

This falls, like so many in New York, splits itself into two distinct sections. The first is a stunning sheer drop from a notch at the top of the gorge, pouring down to a hanging valley. The flow's force pushes on to a second drop, this one a segmented cascade that

Pass Bastion Falls on your way to the Kaaterskill Falls Trail.

falls into a boulder-laden pool directly below. From here the creek continues down the mountain as whitecaps, frills, and the occasional rapid. Plenty of large glacial erratics provide places for you to sit or stand directly in front of the falls, where you can admire the entire phenomenon. The most energetic visitors climb to the falls' second level on a new staircase constructed in 2017, a development that made a trip to the top a safer alternative to the slippery "social trail" used by hikers for decades. (You also have the option of seeing the falls from the top on the North–South Lake Escarpment Trail.)

We don't want to give Bastion Falls short shrift here—this entirely likable falls at the entrance to the Kaaterskill Falls trail provides a sort of aquatic appetizer to the main course farther up. Those who feel that the hike to Kaaterskill may be too strenuous may be satisfied with this impressive cascade that's viewable from the roadside. Be careful if you pull off and get out of your car here; this bend in the road can be a blind corner for cars coming around it from the south.

This hike gets crowded in May and June, even in the middle of the week. We encountered busloads of college students, day campers, retirees, young vacationing couples, families with children, tourists from European countries, an artist and her Jack Russell terrier, and even a trail maintenance crew from the Adirondack Mountain Club—and we were here on a Thursday. Come early in the day or late in the afternoon to get a parking space.

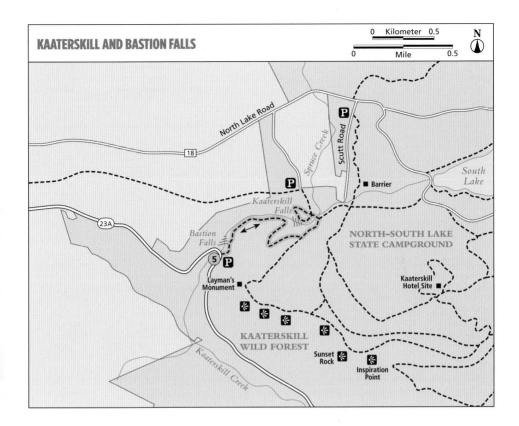

MILES AND DIRECTIONS

0.0 Park in the area provided on the left side of NY 23A West. Cross the road and step over the guardrail to be out of the line of traffic. The road's construction will force you back onto the shoulder for short distances, so stay over to the side as far as you can.

0.3 Arrive at Bastion Falls. The trail to Kaaterskill Falls begins just past Bastion; you'll see a clearly marked trailhead. Begin the ascent, climbing a long series of staircase-like boulders to a wooden staircase. After the stairs, the trail levels off for a bit.

0.4 Climb another wooden staircase. From here the trail follows closely along the creek but is fairly level for a while. Cross a number of small streams on rocks.

0.6 A last scramble and rock-hop takes you to a clear view of the magnificent falls from the bottom. There are plenty of large rock slabs and big boulders here if you want to sit and contemplate the double cascade. You will see the staircase to the top on your right as you face the falls. Take this up.

1.1 Reach the top of the staircase. When you're ready, head back down the way you came. Watch out for wet, slippery rocks as you descend.

1.9 You're back at Bastion Falls. Take a last look before heading back down the road to the parking area.

2.2 Arrive back at the parking area.

6 WEST KILL MOUNTAIN

West Kill is number 6 on the Catskill 3500 Club's high peaks list. It's a challenging hike but worth your time for some of the best views in the region.

County: Greene
Start: Diamond Notch parking lot, Spruceton Road
Elevation gain: 1,786 feet
Distance: 6.2 miles out and back
Difficulty: Difficult
Hiking time: About 4.5 hours
Seasons: Year-round
Schedule: Open daily; camping areas available
Fees and permits: No fees or permits required
Trail contact: DEC Region 4 Stamford Office (Mon through Fri, 8:30 a.m. to 4:30 p.m.); (607) 652-7365; email: r4.ump@dec.ny.gov

Canine compatibility: Dogs permitted on leash
Trail surface: Soil, rocks, roots
Land status: New York State Department of Environmental Conservation
Nearest town: Tannersville, New York
Maps: Catskill Mountaineer West Kill Mountain (catskillmountaineer.com/HWK-westkill.html); New York–New Jersey Trail Conference Trail Map 141
Special considerations: Wear sturdy hiking shoes with good ankle support. Bring crampons for winter or early-spring hiking.

FINDING THE TRAILHEAD

From the New York State Thruway, take exit 21 (Catskill). Drive about 0.75 mile and take a right on NY 23 West. Travel 6.6 miles to Cairo. Turn left on NY 32 and stay on this road for about 7.5 miles. Turn right onto NY 23A and go about 22 miles to the intersection of NY 23A and CR 42. About 0.3 mile past the intersection, head left over the bridge (over Schoharie Creek); you're now on NY 42. Go approximately 4.1 miles to CR 6 (Spruceton Road). Stay on CR 6 for about 7 miles. Along the way it becomes a one-lane road. Keep going. There are three small parking lots not far from the trailhead. (**Note:** Many people park on the road, but it is dangerous; get to the trailhead early to find a legitimate parking spot.) Trailhead GPS: N42 18.238' / W74 26.999'

THE HIKE

Off CR 6, driving along the Spruceton Road to the West Kill trail, the view is picturesque, dotted with horse farms, clapboard churches, neat farmhouses, and rolling hills. You'll glimpse a creek, known as West Kill, in the woods as the road bends and curves. There are so many beautiful creeks in the Catskills, you might not think anything of it, never guessing at this small stream's importance.

Waterways can seem like tree branches, one creek a tributary of another. West Kill is an 11-mile tributary off Schoharie Creek, which is a tributary of the Mohawk River, itself a tributary of the Hudson River. Ultimately, water from West Kill flows into the Schoharie Reservoir, one of nineteen reservoirs that supply water to New York City.

To create the Schoharie Reservoir, in the early 1920s, New York City condemned significant landholdings in the village of Gilboa, New York, evacuated and relocated its residents, and dammed the creek. The reservoir is a 6-mile basin holding 17.6 billion gallons of water, supplying 9 million people with about 15 percent of their water. The

The sounds of rushing water surround you during the first mile of this hike, which runs along West Kill Creek. STACEY FREED

Schoharie is actually one of the smaller New York City reservoirs. (The largest is the Pepacton Reservoir in nearby Delaware County.)

Although this part of the Catskills has flooded many times, in 2011 Hurricane Irene overpowered the region around Margaretville, Gilboa, Roxbury, and Fleischmanns in what is still referred to as a "500-year flood" event. Because of climate change, these types of storms are increasing in frequency.

It's worth keeping the power of water in mind as you traverse the many streams and rivulets running along the West Kill trail as you hike. And always be prepared to get wet; the mountains around the West Kill watershed average 45.2 inches of rain a year, which is high for the region. There are summer downpours, winter rain-on-snow events, and late-summer or early-autumn hurricanes that can sweep through the mountains.

MILES AND DIRECTIONS

0.0 Start from one of the parking lots on Spruceton Road. (The lot on your right is a private lot.) Walk on Spruceton Road to where it dead-ends at the barrier gates to the trail. Follow the blue trail marker for the Diamond Notch Trail (an old carriage road) to begin the hike to West Kill summit. Sign the register a few yards ahead. The path is wide, not very steep, and covered in loose stone. On your right, West Kill rushes down the hill.

0.9 Cross the bridge over the creek. You are at the crossroads of the Diamond Notch Trail and the Devil's Path. Bear right and follow the red trail markers for the Devil's Path in the direction of West Kill Mountain. The terrain is gnarly hardwood roots and small stones but relatively flat for about 0.1 mile. Then a steep rise begins. Soon you'll see the sign (and red trail marker) for "Westkill Mt. Summit, 2.2 miles." Springwater seems to bubble up from nowhere and crisscrosses the trail as you hike; watch your step.

2.2 Just past here is a rock overhang referred to as the "cave." It may look cozy, but don't plan on nesting. If the trees are in "leaf-off" stage, just past here you'll soon begin to see sky through the branches. Expect

One of the few Catskill mountains with an actual marker announcing your arrival at a summit. STACEY FREED

some climbing and scrambling over rocks for the next 0.5 mile or so. Not far from the cave, you'll see the Department of Environmental Conservation 3,500-foot marker. There is no camping above 3,500 feet in the Catskills, and you can't camp within 150 feet of the trail.

A cozy spot to grab some rest and shade before the trail grows steeper. STACEY FREED

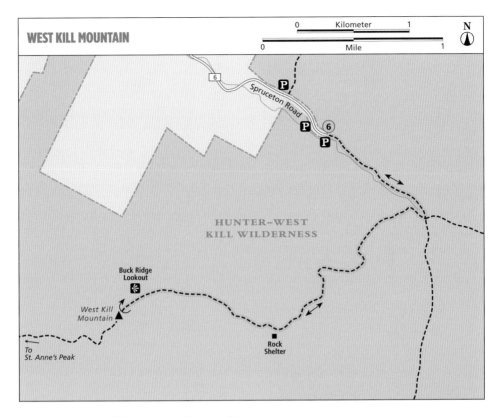

Kilometer

Mile

N

HUNTER–WEST
KILL WILDERNESS

Buck Ridge
Lookout

West Kill
Mountain

To
St. Anne's Peak

Rock
Shelter

2.8 Buck Ridge Lookout, the payoff for this challenging hike. Enjoy the 180-degree view of Hunter Mountain, Plateau, Rusk, Windham High Peak, Caudal, Camel's Hump, Thomas Cole, Black Dome, Blackhead, and Arizona. Off in the distance is Lanesville, New York. If you do a 180, walk through the now slightly overgrown woods a few yards to catch the view of Spruceton Valley on the other side of the ridge. Turn back and continue to the summit by following the red markers and a soft, nearly flat path.

3.1 Reach West Kill summit, 3,898 feet. Unlike many others in the Catskills, this summit has a posted sign. Head back down the trail in the direction you came up.

6.2 Arrive back at the parking lot. **Note:** If you would like a libation reward— and you deserve it after this hike— take the Spruceton Road/CR 6 to West Kill Brewing (2173 Spruceton Rd.), but check their hours first.

Volunteer trail keepers angle rocks to help divert downhill water. STACEY FREED

7 DIBBLE'S QUARRY

Family-friendly hike that ends with your very own bluestone throne to relax in.

County: Greene
Start: Roaring Fork Trailhead
Elevation gain: 340 feet
Distance: 2.0 miles out and back
Difficulty: Easy
Hiking time: About 1.5 hours
Seasons: Year-round
Schedule: Open daily. Camping areas available.
Fees and permits: No fees or permits required
Trail contact: DEC Region 4 · Stamford Office (Mon through Fri, 8:30 a.m. to 4:30 p.m.); (607) 652-7365; email: r4.ump@dec.ny.gov

Canine compatibility: Dogs permitted on leash
Trail surface: Rocks, roots, soil
Land status: New York State Department of Environmental Conservation
Nearest town: Saugerties, New York
Other trail users: Snowshoers (in season); campers
Maps: AllTrails Dibble's Quarry (alltrails.com/explore/recording/dibbles-quarry); New York–New Jersey Trail Conference Trail Map 141
Special considerations: Seasonal streambeds—be prepared for wet terrain.

FINDING THE TRAILHEAD

From the New York State Thruway take exit 20 (Saugerties). Turn left on NY 212/NY 32. At the light make a right onto NY 32 North. Drive 6 miles and continue straight onto NY 32A. Drive another 1.9 miles, turn left onto NY 23A, and head up a winding road toward Tannersville. Turn left onto CR 16/Platte Clove Road and continue about 5 miles. Turn right on Dale Lane and travel about 1.2 miles. The road bears right and the name changes to Roaring Kill Road. Continue until the road dead-ends at the parking area. Get here early; the small lot fills up fast on weekends. People will park on the side of the road. Trailhead GPS: N42 15.111' / W74 13.094'

Note: Dibble's Quarry is not listed on the trailhead sign. Follow the blue-blazed trail for Pecoy Notch.

THE HIKE

The Catskill quarry industry began in Ulster County in the mid-1800s. The tiny grains that make up bluestone (which also comes in green, brown, pink, purple, and red) were deposited in the Catskill Delta 345 to 370 million years ago as part of an ancient sea that covered most of what is now New York State.

Bluestone is durable and resistant to temperature changes and shifts in pressure. It splits relatively easily into layers that can be used as architectural and building stone. In the 1800s it was a good choice for making sidewalks in Manhattan. Quarry workers cleared debris from stone ledges with blasting powder—a dangerous job—then drove wedges between the stone's natural layers to pry free slabs from the rock bed and loaded the slabs onto a wagon. It took as many as sixteen horses to move flats that might be 15 feet wide and 5 inches thick. The loaded wagons could weigh as much as 18 tons.

A doubletrack 18-mile road that could support two wagons at a time ran from the Hurley and Woodstock regions of the Catskills to Kingston. Stonecutters worked on the stones there, and the bluestone was then loaded onto boats and sent down the Hudson River.

Above: At the firepit, a chance to gaze over at Round Top Mountain, Kaaterskill High Peak, and Twin Mountain.
Below: Remnants of Dibble's bluestone quarry let you know you're almost to the summit.

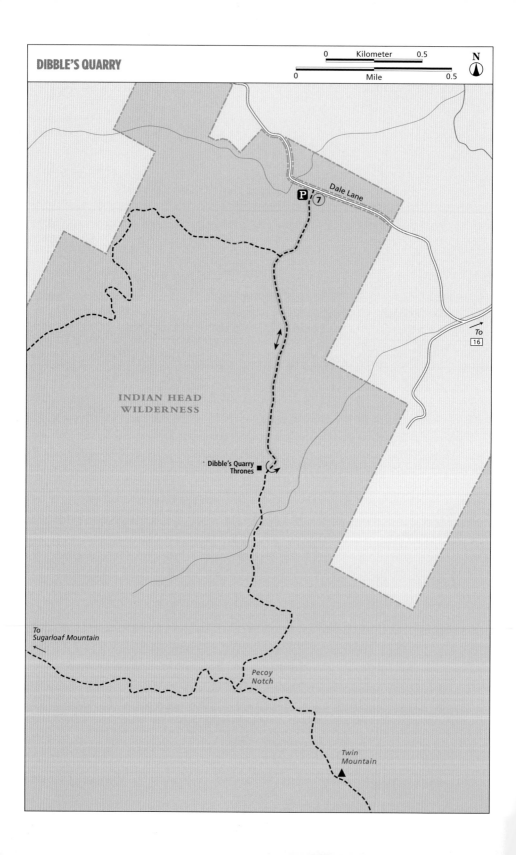

DIBBLE'S QUARRY

0   Kilometer   0.5

0   Mile   0.5

N

Dale Lane

P   7

To 16

INDIAN HEAD
WILDERNESS

Dibble's Quarry
Thrones

To
Sugarloaf Mountain

Pecoy
Notch

Twin
Mountain

Enjoy a snack while sitting on one of the bluestone thrones.

Dibble's Quarry was one of those nineteenth-century quarries, located just a mile from the roadway. As you hike in, you'll walk on reddish claylike soil up a gradual incline snaked by tree roots. About 0.5 mile in you'll see small chairs built by ambitious, and unknown, people. But there's more to come. You'll pass through stands of hemlock and eventually reach the "throne" area with a tall firepit and chairs built for giants. Sitting in these bluestone seats affords a magnificent view of Round Top Mountain, Kaaterskill High Peak, and Twin Mountain. You're facing east, so it's a great spot to watch the sunrise. If you bring children with you, there are lots of little trails and stone walls around the seating area to explore.

MILES AND DIRECTIONS

0.0   Start from the parking lot. The first part of the hike is a connector trail, marked yellow.

0.2   Cross a stream, following the yellow markers.

0.3   Bear left at a trail sign and head toward Pecoy Notch, following the blue markers.

1.0   The trail turns left. Follow blue markers down to the "furniture." Return the way you came. (**Option**: Continue hiking to Pecoy Notch and Sugarloaf Mountain.)

2.0   Arrive back at the parking lot.

8 HUCKLEBERRY POINT TRAIL

This short, relatively easy hike proves that you don't have to scrape the clouds to get a good workout and an amazing payoff: views of Overlook Mountain, peaks in the Indian Head Wilderness, the Ashokan Reservoir—and lots of fresh blueberries if you're there in season.

County: Greene
Start: Steenburg Road parking area, Platte Clove Road (CR 16)
Elevation gain: 644 feet
Distance: 5.0 miles out and back
Difficulty: Easy
Hiking time: About 3 hours
Seasons: Year-round
Schedule: Open daily; camping areas available
Fees and permits: No fees or permits required
Trail contact: DEC Region 4 Stamford Office (Mon through Fri, 8:30 a.m. to 4:30 p.m.); (607) 652-7365; email: r4.ump@dec.ny.gov
Canine compatibility: Dogs permitted on leash
Trail surface: Soil, rocks, roots

Land status: New York State Department of Environmental Conservation
Nearest town: Saugerties, New York
Other trail users: Campers; snowshoers, snowmobilers (in season)
Maps: AllTrails Huckleberry Point (alltrails.com/explore/trail/us/new-york/huckleberry-point-trail?mobileMap=false&ref=sidebar-static-map); New York–New Jersey Trail Conference Trail Map 141
Special considerations: Dress for getting your feet wet; you'll be crossing and recrossing a creek. You may want to skip this hike if there has been a lot of rain; the creek may be impassable.

FINDING THE TRAILHEAD

Take the New York State Thruway to exit 21 (Catskill) and turn left. In 0.5 mile turn right onto NY 23 West and drive about 5 miles. Turn left onto NY 32 and drive about 7.5 miles. Turn right onto NY 23A and drive about 7.5 miles, entering Tannersville. Turn left at the light onto Railroad Avenue (CR 16). This will become Spruce Street and then Platte Clove Road. Take this for about 8 miles, passing Josh Road on your left. Continue another 0.5 mile to the DEC parking lot on your left. (If you start going down the hill to the valley, you've gone too far. The downhill section of the road is closed Nov 1 to Apr 15.) Trailhead GPS: N42 13.307' / W74 08.173'

Note: Do not block the gate entrance at the parking lot; there is a house at the end of this road. Also, do not drive up the dirt entrance road to the trailhead; it is private property.

THE HIKE

For a region with trails that are deeply shaded by tree cover, the Catskill Mountains are home to a surprising number of colorful flowers and hundreds of species of plants. In spring there's everything from sweet cicely to saxifrage, hobble bush, violets, yellow rocket, golden Alexander, eastern red columbine, purple gaywings, pink lady's slipper, and more. Summer features all types of berries and clover and milkweed. Even autumn has its beauties in asters, goldenrod, and bergamot.

The Huckleberry Trail, of course, has huckleberries, which resemble blueberries. In some parts of the country people refer to huckleberries as blueberries and vice versa, but they are different species. In the western United States, huckleberries grow singly, while

Plan to get wet on this hike as you cross and recross creeks.

blueberries grow in clusters. In the East, huckleberries do grow in clusters, but huckle-berry plants don't like to be domesticated (unlike the blueberries you can grow in your backyard), and they yield less fruit than blueberry plants. None of this matters to black bears, whose paths you might cross while hiking. Foraging like anteaters, they nose in and eat up to 30,000 berries in a good year.

As you hike to Huckleberry Point, the trail crosses Plattekill Creek and winds through swaths of ferns and myriad birch trees as well as black cherry, chestnut oak, and beech. You'll wander through a pine forest, the air redolent with their fragrance. You may find a few sugar maples. In early spring, with few leaves on the trees, you'll be treated to ephem-eral flowers like lady's slippers. In mid-spring, the trail, full of blooming mountain laurel, is a magical place. If you arrive at the point in summer, be sure to sample the incredibly flavorful lowbush wild blueberries.

As you take in the vista, you may also get an air show—turkey vultures and red-tailed hawks riding the thermals, a kind of atmospheric updraft caused by heat rising from the earth's surface.

MILES AND DIRECTIONS

0.0 Start at the trail register next to a metal gate. Sign in and begin following the blue-marked trail (Long Path). You will also see red markers for the snowmobile trail. The trail inclines gradually.

0.71 The trail veers to the right; follow the blue trail markers. If you continue straight, you will hit a private hunting camp.

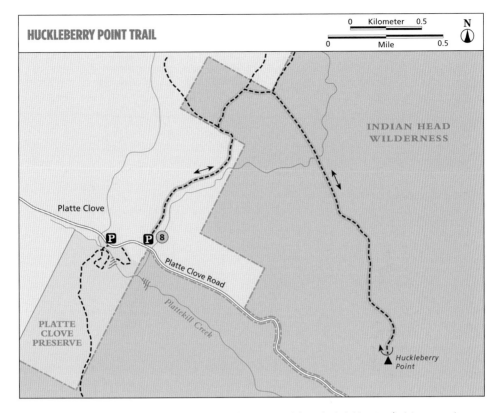

0   Kilometer   0.5

0   Mile   0.5

N

INDIAN HEAD
WILDERNESS

Platte Clove

8

Platte Clove Road

Plattekill Creek

PLATTE
CLOVE
PRESERVE

Huckleberry
Point

0.95 Continue on the blue-blazed trail. On your right, a helpful hunter/cabin owner has placed a giant handwritten sign telling you that the trail bears right. Follow it.

1.1 Bear right onto the yellow-marked trail. (The blue-blazed trail heads north to Kaaterskill High Peak, part of the Long Path.) Keep your eyes peeled for the yellow markers in order to remain on the trail, but also keep your eyes peeled for all the roots you will be walking over.

1.3 Cross Plattekill Creek over large stones. (***Caution:*** Don't attempt to cross this after heavy rains.)

1.4 Begin a steep ascent, which levels out in around 0.3 mile.

2.0 At the crest of the rise, there's a field of mountain laurel; if you're here early enough in the season the whole field will be filled with pinkish-white flowers.

2.1 Begin a steep downhill.

2.5 You've reached Huckleberry Point. (There's a social trail just before the point that leads to a small clearing with a firepit and large bluestone rocks set up as a seating area.) Turn around and return the way you came.

5.0 Arrive back at the gate and trail register.

Time it right in mid-spring and fields of mountain laurel greet you.

9 PLATTEKILL PRESERVE FALLS

A hidden gorge, carved deep by rushing water and glacial activity, masks a glorious horsetail falls.

County: Greene
Start: Parking area for the Long Path at the Platte Clove Wilderness Preserve, marked with a wooden NYSDEC sign for the Snowmobile Trail
Elevation gain: 155 feet
Distance: 0.6 mile out and back
Difficulty: Moderate
Hiking time: About 40 minutes
Seasons: Spring and summer
Schedule: Open daily, sunrise to sunset
Fees and permits: None
Trail contact: The Catskill Center for Conservation and Development, NY

28, Arkville 12406; (845) 586-2611; catskillcenter.org
Canine compatibility: Dogs permitted on leash
Trail surface: Dirt and rock path
Land status: Platte Clove Wilderness Preserve; open to the public
Nearest town: Palenville, New York
Other trail users: Thru-hikers on the Long Path
Maps: *DeLorme: New York State Atlas & Gazetteer:* Page 97
Special considerations: The trail is steep and slippery, even in dry weather—we don't recommend this one for winter or early-spring hiking.

FINDING THE TRAILHEAD

From the junction of West Saugerties and Manorville Roads in West Saugerties, drive west on West Saugerties Road for 1 mile until it becomes Platte Clove Road. Continue on Platte Clove Road for 1.5 miles to the Platte Clove Wilderness Preserve, on your left. Park at the trailhead for the Long Path, marked with a wooden NYSDEC sign for the Snowmobile Trail. Trailhead GPS: N42 07.991' / W74 05.175'

THE HIKE

Somehow this 208-acre preserve managed to retain its natural state through centuries of timber production and bluestone mining in the surrounding Catskill Mountain region—and for this, hikers everywhere should be grateful. Enlightened members of the Griswold family deeded Platte Clove Preserve to the Catskill Center for Conservation and Development back in 1975, and since then the center's staff and volunteers have worked to keep this gem open to the public for limited use. You are welcome to hike here, but mountain bikes and horses are strictly prohibited. Once you see the rocky, steeply pitched path to the falls, these rules will make a great deal of sense.

Your progress down the path reveals a great deal about the geological forces that shaped this valley (or "clove"). Erosion and the Platte Kill's force through this heavily wooded area dug a channel through the mountains, gradually widening it to form a streambed. This process was well under way when glaciers arrived with the most recent ice age, gouging the stream's channel into the deeply slanted V you see today. Several other waterfalls drop over glacially carved precipices downstream from here—there's no safe path to these at this time—and the movement of the huge bodies of ice dragged large boulders, known as "glacial erratics," into the streambed.

Platte Clove Preserve invites visitors to hike into its depths.

The falls come into view as you arrive at the bottom of the gorge, a magnificently arc-ing horsetail that rains gracefully down to a surprisingly peaceful plunge pool. The rock faces gleaming with water and sunlight, the thick moss and hanging gardens on the gorge walls, and the myriad places to sit and contemplate the spectacle will encourage you to linger here before making the fairly tough trek back up to your vehicle.

MILES AND DIRECTIONS

0.0 Start from the parking area, pass the chain across the beginning of the gravel drive, and walk down the drive, past the red house. Follow the Platte Clove Preserve Hik-ing Trail. The path turns right into the woods at the top of a long slope. Follow the path downhill for 0.2 mile.

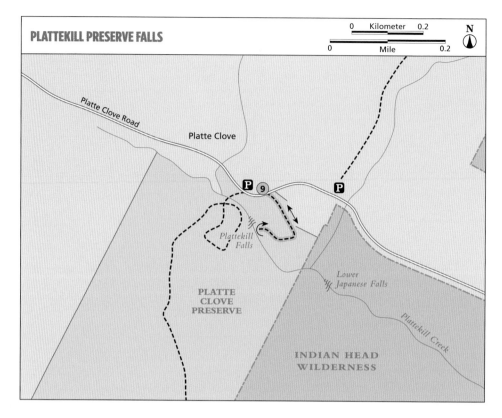

PLATTEKILL PRESERVE FALLS

0.2   The path makes a careful cross on the edge of a hill just before you arrive at an area strewn with large rocks. Scramble over these rocks until you reach your desired view of the falls.

0.3   Enjoy the falls in full view. It begins as a short tumble and then arches away from the gorge wall to the pool below. When you're ready, make your way back up the long slope to the beginning of the trail.

0.6   Arrive back at the parking area.

10 CODFISH POINT

If you don't have a great deal of time and want a moderate hike with a little challenge, this one brings you to a lovely view of the Hudson Valley.

County: Greene
Start: Platte Clove Road (CR 16)
Elevation gain: 650 feet
Distance: 4.6 miles out and back
Difficulty: Moderate
Hiking time: About 2 hours
Seasons: Year-round
Schedule: Open daily. Camping areas available.
Fees and permits: No fees or permits required
Trail contact: Catskills Visitor Center, 5096 NY 28, Mount Tremper 12457; (845) 688-3369

Canine compatibility: Dogs permitted on leash
Trail surface: Soil, roots, rocks
Land status: New York State Department of Environmental Conservation
Nearest town: Saugerties, New York
Other trail users: Campers
Maps: AllTrails Codfish Point (alltrails .com/explore/trail/us/new-york/ codfish-point-trail?mobileMap=fa lse&ref=sidebar-static-map); New York–New Jersey Trail Conference Trail Map 141

FINDING THE TRAILHEAD

Take the New York State Thruway to exit 21 (Catskill). Turn left and in 0.5 mile turn right onto NY 23 West. Continue about 5 miles and turn left onto NY 32. Drive about 7.5 miles and turn right onto NY 23A. Continue about 7.5 miles, entering Tannersville. Turn left at the light onto Railroad Avenue (CR 16). This will become Spruce Street and then Platte Clove Road. Travel about 8 miles, passing Josh Road on your left. Go another 0.5 mile to the DEC parking lot on your left. (If you start going down the hill to the valley, you have gone too far. The downhill section of the road is closed Nov 1 to Apr 15.) Leave the parking lot, turn right, cross the street, and head 0.21 mile to the trailhead, on your left. Trailhead GPS: N42 13.383' / W74 08.197'

THE HIKE

The Platte Clove Wilderness Preserve, in the northeast region of the Catskills, is more than 200 acres filled with waterfalls and trails. The land was donated to the Catskill Center by the Griswold family in 1975 for the permanent protection of the flora, fauna, and geological and historical features present on the property.

The main spine trail to Codfish Point is known as the Overlook Trail, which extends from Platte Clove (a Dutch word meaning "cleave," as a valley would) to the summit of Overlook Mountain, near Woodstock, New York. Many of the trails in these woods are old carriage roads that once gave visitors access to the Overlook Mountain House.

Before heading out on your Codfish Point hike, it's worth taking the 0.3-mile Waterfall Trail, which begins at the entrance to the Platte Clove Wilderness Preserve.

Before turning right onto the trailhead to Codfish Point, you'll see a small red house that was once used by the Catskill Center for Conservation for its artist in residence program. This program was discontinued in early 2022, and the house is not open to the public.

Take in the view of the Hudson Valley on a clear day.

You have several hiking choices at the Platte Clove entrance: Take the trail to Codfish Point and return to the parking area (4.6 miles out and back). Or, after visiting Codfish Point, return to the trail and continue to Echo Lake (8.8 miles out and back, if you include the falls loop at the beginning of the hike) and then to Overlook Mountain (13.0 miles out and back). You can even do this all as an overnight—there are several camping spots along the way.

You might try that longer hike as a shuttle with two vehicles. Park one vehicle at Meads Mountain Road in Woodstock, across the street from the Karma Triyana Dharmachakra monastery. Then, with your other vehicle, take a 25-minute drive to the Platte Clove Road trailhead entrance.

But just heading out and back to Codfish Point is a satisfying hike that offers a great view of the Hudson Valley—and you can enjoy the vista perched on a bluestone "easy chair."

MILES AND DIRECTIONS

0.0   Start at the entrance to the Platte Clove Wilderness Preserve.

0.1   Sign in at the register. The trail will be marked with aqua-colored Long Path markers and blue diamond markers of the Platte Clove Preserve. Turn left over the kingpost bridge and follow the blue markers.

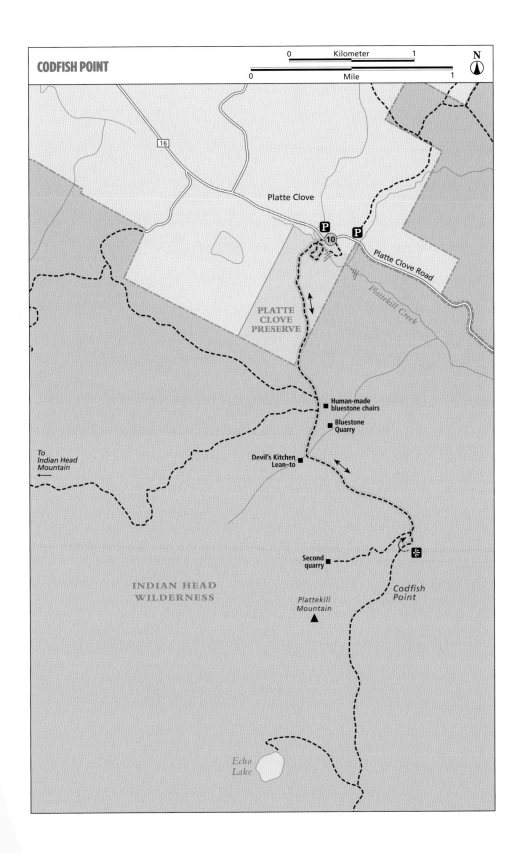

CODFISH POINT

0   Kilometer   1

0   Mile   1

N

16

Platte Clove

P 10 P

Platte Clove Road

Plattekill Creek

PLATTE
CLOVE
PRESERVE

Human-made
bluestone chairs

Bluestone
Quarry

To
Indian Head
Mountain

Devil's Kitchen
Lean–to

Second
quarry

Codfish
Point

INDIAN HEAD
WILDERNESS

Plattekill
Mountain

Echo
Lake

Where there's bluestone, there is furniture.

0.37 Begin a gradual incline. The trail is covered with roots and rocks.

1.0 Look left through the trees to see the remnants of a bluestone quarry. Enterprising folks have created sturdy stone slab "furniture" to sit on.

1.15 On your left are signs directing you to the Devil's Kitchen lean-to and the continuance of the blue-marked trail. Some of the trail is marked by blue and red markers. Follow the blue markers.

1.23 On the right is the path to Indian Head and Mink Hollow. Continue on the blue-marked trail toward the Devil's Kitchen lean-to.

1.45 Devil's Kitchen lean-to, with creek on your left. Stay on the blue-marked trail. A few yards ahead, cross the small wooden bridge over a creek.

2.2 Come to an intersection with a yellow-marked trail. Bear left on the yellow-marked trail to head to Codfish Point. The trail will slope gently down, and on your left you'll see the view through breaks in the trees.

2.3 Reach Codfish Point. Check out the view of the Hudson Valley. A short distance off to the right is an abandoned bluestone quarry. Turn back onto the blue-marked trail to return to the parking lot.

4.6 Arrive back at the parking lot.

11 ECHO LAKE

A chance to enjoy a serene spot for camping and fishing in the heart of the mountains.

County: Ulster
Start: Platte Clove Road (CR 16)
Elevation gain: 1,532 feet
Distance: 7.4 miles out and back
Difficulty: Moderate
Hiking time: About 3.5 hours
Seasons: Year-round
Schedule: Open daily; camping areas available
Fees and permits: No fees or permits required
Trail contact: DEC Region 3 New Paltz Office; (845) 256-3076; email: r3forestry@dec.ny.gov
Canine compatibility: Dogs permitted on leash

Trail surface: Soil, roots, rocks
Land status: New York State Department of Environmental Conservation
Nearest town: Woodstock, New York
Other trail users: Snowshoers, cross-country skiers (in season)
Maps: AllTrails Echo Lake (all trails.com/explore/trail/us/new-york/echo-lake?mobileMap=false&ref=sidebar-static-map); New York–New Jersey Trail Conference Trail Map 141
Special considerations: Stay alert for rattlesnakes and water snakes.

FINDING THE TRAILHEAD

 Take the New York State Thruway to exit 21 (Catskill). Turn left and in 0.5 mile turn right onto NY 23 West and drive about 5 miles. Turn left onto NY 32 and continue about 7.5 miles. Turn right onto NY 23A and drive about 7.5 miles, entering Tannersville. Turn left at the light onto Railroad Avenue (CR 16). This will become Spruce Street and then Platte Clove Road. Take this for about 8 miles, passing Josh Road on your left. Continue another 0.5 mile to the DEC parking lot on your left. (If you start going down the hill to the valley, you have gone too far. The downhill section of the road is closed Nov 1 to Apr 15.) Leave the parking lot, turn right, cross the street, and head 0.21 mile to the trailhead, which is on your left. Trailhead GPS: N42 13.382' / W74 08.196'

THE HIKE

Aside from hiking, it's great to swim, fish, or camp in the Catskills, and there are plenty of places to choose from.

Myriad waterfalls, creeks, streams, lakes, rivers, swimming holes, and ponds dot the park. Near the Giant Ledge Trail parking area there's Otter Falls; the Sundown Wild Forest has Peekamoose Blue Hole; not far from the Escarpment Trail in the Windham Blackhead Range Wilderness there's Colgate Lake; and so many others. (Learn more about swimming opportunities in the Catskills by visiting the Catskills Visitor Center at 5096 NY 28 in Mount Tremper.)

As for camping, there are a few rules: You aren't allowed to camp within 150 feet of any trail, water source, or road. No camping next to a lean-to, and no camping above 3,500 feet during spring, summer, and fall. As you hike, you'll find trail markers directing you to camping areas, many of which include large lean-tos and firepits.

Echo Lake is the source of the Sawkill River, the main body of water that runs through the town of Woodstock. Located in the Indian Head Wilderness between Plattekill and

This serene spot can only be accessed by a long hike. Several campsites ring the lake.

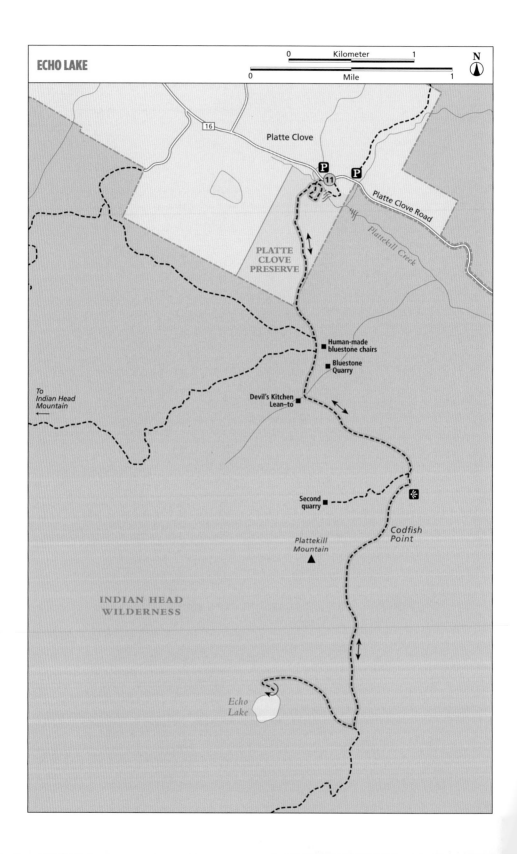

Overlook Mountains, Echo Lake can be murky and buggy and a haven for beavers, but it's still a nice spot for a dip. It's also a great place for camping or fishing. The lake has a self-sustaining population of wild brook trout. There is a large lean-to and seven designated campsites near the lake. And the only way to get here is to hike in.

The lake has brook trout, but beavers and snakes are also fans of the location.

MILES AND DIRECTIONS

0.0 Start at the entrance to the Platte Clove Wilderness Preserve.

0.1 Sign in at the register. The trail will be marked with aqua-colored Long Path markers and blue diamond markers of the Platte Clove Preserve. Turn left over the kingpost bridge and follow the blue markers.

0.37 Begin a gradual incline. The trail is covered with roots and rocks.

1.0 Look left through the trees to see the remnants of a bluestone quarry. Enterprising folks have created sturdy stone slab "furniture" to sit on.

1.15 On your left are signs directing you to the Devil's Kitchen lean-to and the continuance of the blue-blazed trail. Some of the trail is marked by blue and red markers. Follow the blue markers.

1.23 On the right is the path to Indian Head and Mink Hollow. Continue on the blue-blazed trail toward the Devil's Kitchen lean-to.

1.45 Devil's Kitchen lean-to, with a creek on your left. Stay on the blue-marked trail. A few yards ahead, cross the small wooden bridge over a creek.

2.2 Come to an intersection with a yellow-blazed trail. Stay on the blue trail. If you bear left on yellow-blazed trail, you can detour to Codfish Point, just 0.1 mile away.

3.7 Sign for the yellow-blazed trail and Echo Lake. Turn right, following the yellow markers for about 0.5 mile. The trail is a fairly steep and very rocky downhill hike to the lake. There's a lean-to and spacious campsites. Turn around and head back up the hill. Turn left to return to the parking lot.

7.4 Arrive back at the parking lot.

THE KINGPOST

Near the trailhead you'll cross Platte Kill Creek via a "kingpost bridge," a type of bridge design defined by a central vertical beam (or kingpost). This 30-foot span (pictured on page 49) has angled support beams supporting the kingpost.

Built originally in the 1870s, the bridge was used by wagons hauling timber and bluestone and by horse-drawn carriages carrying guests to and from the Plattekill Falls House, the Overlook Mountain House, and other hotels and boardinghouses.

Through a partnership between the Catskill Center and the New York–New Jersey Trail Conference, volunteers constructed the bridge on its original stone abutments in 2001. It was likely the first time in more than one hundred years that a wooden kingpost bridge had been built in the Catskills.

Along with the bridge installation, a new hiking trail was blazed and designated part of the Long Path.

12 OVERLOOK MOUNTAIN

One of the top three most-visited locations in the Catskill Forest Preserve. Go for the history—stay for the views.

County: Ulster
Start: Meads Mountain Road parking lot, across the street from Karma Triyana Dharmachakra monastery
Elevation gain: 1,397 feet
Distance: 4.6 miles out and back
Difficulty: Moderate; can be strenuous at times
Hiking time: About 3.5 hours
Seasons: Year-round
Schedule: Open daily; camping areas available
Fees and permits: No fees or permits required
Trail contact: DEC Region 3 New Paltz Office; (845) 256-3076; email: r3forestry@dec.ny.gov

Canine compatibility: Dogs permitted on leash
Trail surface: Gravel, roots, rocks
Land status: New York State Department of Environmental Conservation
Nearest town: Woodstock, New York
Other trail users: Campers; snowshoers, cross-country skiers (in season)
Maps: Catskill Mountaineer Overlook Mountain and Echo Lake (catskillmountaineer.com/IH-overlook.html); New York–New Jersey Trail Conference Trail Map 141
Special considerations: Be prepared for rattlesnakes on the trail.

FINDING THE TRAILHEAD

From the New York State Thruway, take exit 19 (Kingston). Keep right onto NY 28W. Stay on 28W approximately 6 miles to a right on NY 375 then eventually a left onto NY 212 to the Woodstock Village Green. At the village green, in the center of town, turn right on Rock City Road, continuing past the four-corners intersection to Meads Mountain Road. The parking lot is on your right about 2 miles up Meads Mountain Road.

Alternately, take I-87 exit 20 (Saugerties) to NY 212 west to the Woodstock Village Green; then follow the above directions. (***Note:*** Get to the Meads Mountain Road parking lot early in the day to ensure a spot.) Trailhead GPS: N42 07.109' / W74 12.266'

THE HIKE

Well before its Borscht Belt popularity, the Catskills drew naturalists, artists, thinkers, and the well-heeled looking for a connection to nature. In the 1800s, investors took advantage of the interest as well as the Catskills' proximity to New York City to build hotels and inns. The top of Overlook Mountain was a particularly popular spot, and over the years three different, opulent hotels were built on the same property. The first two succumbed to fire; the third version, the Overlook Mountain House, built in the 1920s, never really got up a head of steam.

For the final version, Morris Newgold, owner of the Times Square Hotel in NYC and of the Mountain House's second iteration, had concrete and other materials hauled up from Woodstock—no more fires for him. But the hotel succumbed to the vagaries of the economy and world events; it was still unfinished in 1939 when Newgold died. His grandson Gabriel took over but soon was called to fight in World War II. When he returned, he'd found the buildings had been vandalized or destroyed.

Above: Horse-drawn carriages brought guests to and from nearby hotels and boardinghouses over this kingpost bridge, built originally in the 1870s.
Below: The ruins of the once-grand Overlook Mountain House bring to mind an earlier era of luxury and romance.

This is one of only five remaining fire towers in the Catskills. Climb the 60-foot tower for a spectacular view.

The castle-like ruins that greet you today as you reach the top of the long gravel road are somehow still grand. Even as nature is reclaiming the massive stone arches and stairs, it's easy to imagine morning walks in the woods, lazy afternoons in the forest filled with dappled sunshine, and evening cocktails and sunset views. Once you've had your fill of romantic visions, make your way to the nearby fire tower, at an elevation of 3,140 feet.

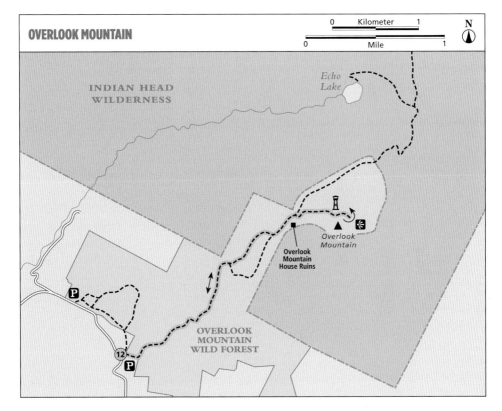

OVERLOOK MOUNTAIN

0 Kilometer 1

0 Mile 1

N

INDIAN HEAD WILDERNESS

Echo Lake

Overlook Mountain House Ruins

Overlook Mountain

OVERLOOK MOUNTAIN WILD FOREST

12

Climb the 60-foot tower, in operation from 1950 to 1988, for a magnificent view of the Berkshire Mountains, the Hudson River, the Ashokan Reservoir, the Shawangunk and Catskill Mountains, and, on a clear day, up to seven states.

MILES AND DIRECTIONS

0.0 Start from the parking lot. Sign in at the register and begin the gradual but lengthy climb up the gravel-and-dirt carriage road (the Overlook Spur Trail).

1.1 The dirt road splits; bear to the left.

1.8 Pass a radio tower and begin to see the ruins of the Overlook Mountain House. Follow the yellow-blazed trail. Beware of rattlesnakes; they like to hang out on the rocks.

2.3 Reach the fire tower, picnic tables, and a small hut usually staffed by a knowledgeable volunteer. Climb the 60-foot tower for a magnificent—but windy—view of the Hudson River Valley and central Catskills. After enjoying the view, return the way you came.

4.6 Arrive back at the parking lot.

ALTERNATIVE ROUTE

You can also get to the Mountain House and fire tower from the opposite direction by parking at the Platte Clove Road trailhead. Although the hike is much longer (13.0 miles out and back), you get to wander through woods rather than hike up a long, steep gravel road.

13 OPUS 40

This repurposing of a bluestone quarry as a permanent art installation has become a world-renowned landmark.

County: Ulster
Start: Visitor center at 356 George Sickle Rd. in Saugerties
Elevation gain: 165 feet
Distance: 0.7-mile loop
Difficulty: Easy
Hiking time: About 1 hour
Seasons: Apr through fall
Schedule: Apr and May, Fri through Mon, 10 a.m. to 5 p.m. (closed Tues through Thurs); summer, Thurs through Mon, 11 a.m. to 5 p.m.
Fees and permits: Admission fee required, discounts for seniors and students, no charge for children age 4 and under
Trail contact: Opus 40 Sculpture Park, 356 George Sickle Rd., Saugerties 12477; (845) 246-3400; opus40.org; email: info@opus40.org
Canine compatibility: Service dogs only
Trail surface: Bluestone, dirt paths
Land status: Owned by Opus 40 Sculpture Park and Museum
Nearest town: Saugerties, New York
Other trail users: Families with children, art lovers
Maps: Available only at the visitor center
Special considerations: Opus 40 closes in the event of major storms. If the weather is questionable, call before visiting.

FINDING THE TRAILHEAD

From Kingston, take Old Kings Highway (US 209) north for about 12 miles to Sheehan Lane. Turn left on Sheehan and continue to Schoolhouse Road; turn right. Continue to John Carle Road and turn right. Take John Carle to the Glasco Turnpike (NY 32); turn left and continue to George Sickle Road. Turn right and watch for the signs for Opus 40, which will be on your left. Trailhead GPS: N42 03.094' / W74 01.872'

THE HIKE

The Catskills have a long and storied history in the world of American art, especially through the works of Hudson River School artists like Thomas Cole and Frederic Edwin Church, Jervis McEntee, Susie Barstow, Eliza Pratt Greatorex, and Julie Hart Beers. These artists made their names by committing the region's landscapes to canvas, but they also opened the door to many other artists who worked in other media—including the effort to make the environment itself a work of art.

Harvey Fite, a professor of sculpture and founder of the theater department at Bard College, bought himself a 6.5-acre rock quarry in 1938. It was not his initial intention to turn the entire property into a sculpture—in fact, he expected to create much smaller works with this virtually limitless supply of feldspathic greywacke, colloquially known as bluestone—but shortly after the purchase, he spent a season restoring Mayan ruins in Honduras. This experience dramatically changed his perspective about the long-term durability and remarkable potential of this malleable stone, and he began to create enormous sculptures on his new property.

It took Fite and his wife, Barbara, some thirty-seven years to construct the imposing structures they called Opus 40, named for the number of years they expected to spend building their masterwork. Harvey Fite actually perished in 1976 in a fall while he was working on the sculpture, cutting short his time to finish it, but as his stepson, writer Jonathan Richards, noted, "Opus 40 is as complete as it ever would have been."

More of a stroll than a hike, a visit to Opus 40 nonetheless delivers some athletic benefit, as it takes physical dexterity to navigate the ramps, terraces, ledges, bridges, and fountains that make this massive project visually fascinating. Wander the labyrinth-like sculpture for as long as you like; then follow the trail through the surrounding woods to see bits of the quarry itself, as well as the birds and small furry animals that inhabit these woodlands.

MILES AND DIRECTIONS

0.0 Start from the parking area and proceed to the stone steps. At the top of the steps, you will find Harvey and Barbara Fite's memorial stones. (They are not buried here; both were cremated.) From here, enter the sculpture. Spend as much time as you like climbing about and enjoying both the craftsmanship and the views from the sculpture's higher points.

0.1 A monolith marks the high point of the sculpture.

The complexity of Opus 40 becomes obvious the first time you see it.

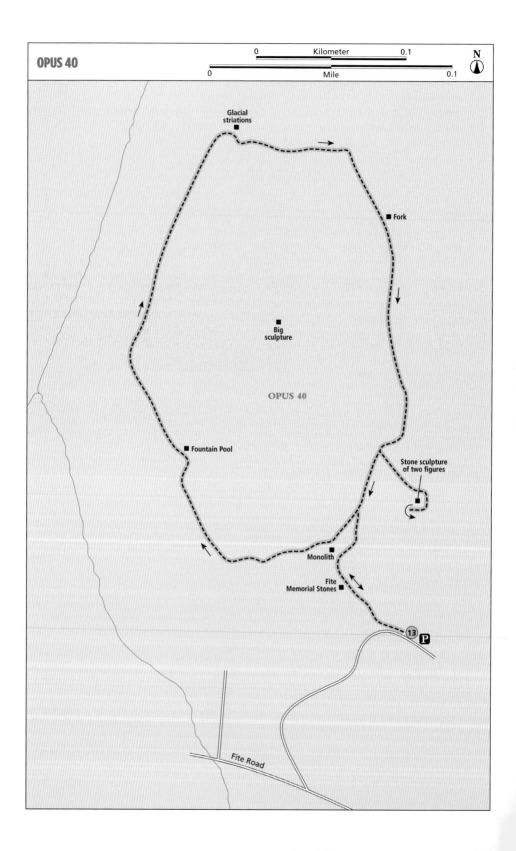

OPUS 40

0 Kilometer 0.1
0 Mile 0.1

N

Glacial
striations

Fork

Big
sculpture

OPUS 40

Fountain Pool

Stone sculpture
of two figures

Monolith

Fite
Memorial Stones

13 P

Fite Road

Climbing around the sculptures, terraces, ledges, stairways, and ramps can be physically challenging.

0.2 At the Fountain Pool on the southwest end of the sculpture, a path to the right leads back into the sculpture for more exploration. Another path leads straight and into the woods. This is the Quarry Trail Loop you will see on the map you received with your tickets. Go straight.

0.3 As you circle the property on the trail through the woods, you will come to large glacial striations (a big area of flat rock). The trail continues to the right; a dirt road goes left. Go right to continue through the woods.

0.4 Come to a fork in the road and bear right to stay on the Quarry Trail Loop. Continue to the stone steps.

0.6 End your walk by returning to the parking area near the Quarryman's Museum.

0.7 Arrive back at the parking area.

14 BLUESTONE WILD FOREST: ONTEORA LAKE

A small mountain lake serves as the centerpiece for this Catskills highlight, a former mining area now blanketed by fragrant forest.

County: Ulster
Start: Trailhead kiosk in the parking area at end of a gravel road off NY 28
Elevation gain: 145 feet—repeatedly on this very hilly trail
Distance: 3.3-mile lollipop
Difficulty: Moderate
Hiking time: About 1.75 hours
Seasons: Spring through fall
Schedule: Open daily, dawn to dusk
Fees and permits: No fees or permits required
Trail contact: New York Department of Environmental Conservation, 625 Broadway, Albany 12223; (516) 402-9405; e-mail: LF.Lands@dec.ny.gov
Canine compatibility: Dogs permitted on leash
Trail surface: Dirt, woodland detritus
Land status: New York State Department of Environmental Conservation
Nearest town: Kingston, New York
Other trail users: Hikers only
Maps: AllTrails Onteora Lake (alltrails.com/trail/us/new-york/onteora-lake-trail)

FINDING THE TRAILHEAD

From Kingston take NY 28 west for about 4 miles. Watch for the New York Department of Environmental Conservation (DEC) sign on your right just after the house at 904 NY 28 and just before the convenience store. Turn right onto the gravel road across from the sign and drive to the parking area. The kiosk marking the trailhead is easy to spot. Trailhead GPS: N41 58.899' / W74 05.160'

THE HIKE

This fairly challenging hike looks deceptively simple at the outset. A well-maintained path leads to a satisfying view of Onteora Lake, with picnic tables and benches for your viewing and noshing enjoyment. Follow the trail into the woods, however, and you'll find plenty of ups and downs through the hills, peppered with dark rock faces that jut from the hillsides. You'll have ample opportunity to examine the bluestone for which this area is famous, as well as an impressive variety of fungi nestled between tree roots along the edges of the trail.

What is bluestone, and why did it serve as a boom product in the mid–1800s? This bluish sandstone found throughout the Catskill Mountains was much in demand as a paving material because it stood up to the elements and offered an attractive slate-gray surface. Bluestone from the Catskills can be found in the base of the Statue of Liberty, in the Empire State Building, and in sidewalks and curbs throughout upstate New York and across the country.

This quarry outside Kingston sent the durable stone into the world on wagons pulled by teams of horses, bringing it to towns along the river for cutting and shaping to order. Stones ground and polished into curb and sidewalk blocks traveled up and down the river to the canals or to the ocean, moving swiftly (by nineteenth-century standards) to contractors across the country.

This all came to an abrupt end, however, with the development in 1880 of Portland cement. Made from limestone, shale, and other materials found in abundant supply across the country, the powdered cement product turned out to be so low cost that it became immensely popular in a very short time. The bluestone mining operations soon went silent as Portland cement grew to dominate the paving and foundation construction market.

You can see the remains of bluestone mining operations as you follow this trail. Great slabs of fissured and chiseled rock punctuate the landscape among the hemlock, red maple, pine, and other trees that now cover the hillsides.

Wildlife also abounds in this forest, so keep an eye open for eastern cottontails, gray and red squirrels, eastern chipmunks, white-tailed deer, and even a glimpse of a beaver. You'll see evidence of beaver activity along the lakeshore in

You'll see evidence of beaver activity on the shores of Onteora Lake.

the form of trunks gnawed down to cone-shaped points and poised to fall with the next big wind. Two large beaver lodges stand in the lake, but the critters themselves are nocturnal, so chances are you'll only spot one if you happen to be hiking at dusk.

Use your ears to pick out the sounds of woodland warblers and vireos in spring and summer, as well as several species of woodpecker, white-breasted and red-breasted nuthatches, gray catbird, blue jay, northern cardinal, and many other year-round birds. Watch the ground for rustling leaves that can indicate wood and hermit thrushes, white-crowned and white-throated sparrows, and American robins in the warmer months.

MILES AND DIRECTIONS

0.0 Start from the kiosk and walk north on the trail. Almost immediately you'll see a side trail to a picnic table at the lake. Stop to admire the lake, then continue straight. The log-lined trail ends at the lake; just before that, a gravel trail goes left. Take the gravel trail.

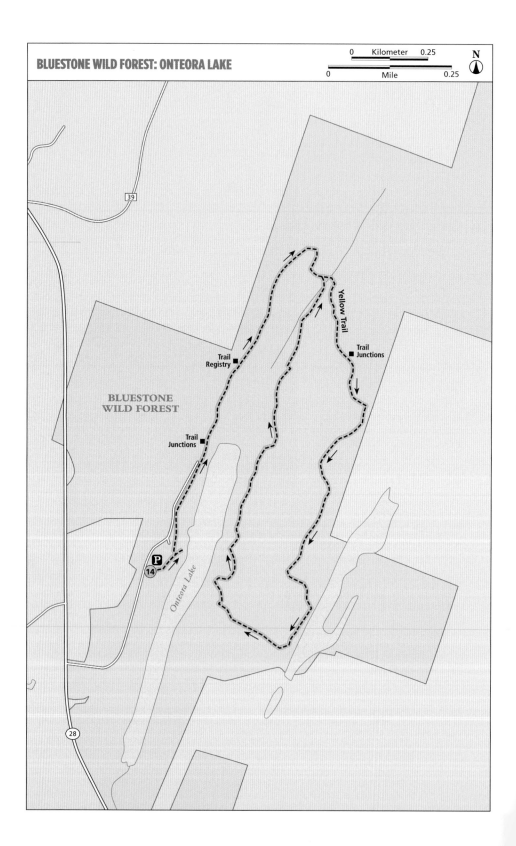

0   Kilometer   0.25

0   Mile   0.25

N

39

Yellow Trail

Trail Junctions

Trail Registry

BLUESTONE WILD FOREST

Trail Junctions

P
14

Onteora Lake

28

Exposed faces of bluestone are all that remain of the mining days near Onteora Lake.

0.3 Another trail joins from the left. Continue straight. The trail begins to climb through the woods.

0.5 Stop at the trail registry and register.

0.8 Watch for yellow markers at the beginning of the loop trail. Take the yellow-blazed trail.

1.0 The red-blazed trail begins to the left at a sign that says, "Forest Preserve Parking." Continue straight on the yellow-blazed trail. On this stretch you can see sheared rock faces where bluestone mining took place.

1.1 The trail makes an emphatic right turn. Keep an eye out for some fascinating fungi through this damp, rocky stretch.

1.5 Reach the edge of the lake. The trail continues straight through the woods along the water then heads up into the woods with a water view. Watch for evidence of beaver activity.

2.5 Rejoin the main trail. Turn left to return to the parking area.

3.3 Arrive back at the parking area.

15 ASHOKAN RESERVOIR PROMENADE AND RAIL TRAIL

Glorious Catskill views for everyone at every age and stage of life.

County: Ulster
Start: Olivebridge Dam trailhead
Elevation gain: 367 feet
Distance: 5.0 miles out and back for the promenade
Difficulty: Easy
Hiking time: About 1.75 hours
Seasons: Year-round
Schedule: Open daily; camping areas available
Fees and permits: No fees or permits required
Trail contact: Catskills Visitor Center, 5096 NY 28, Mount Tremper 12457; (845) 688-3369; email: info@catskillcenter.org
Canine compatibility: Dogs permitted on leash

Trail surface: Paved road
Land status: New York City Department of Environmental Protection, reservoir lands
Nearest town: Woodstock, New York
Other trail users: Runners, cross-country skiers, cyclists, in-line skaters
Maps: New York–New Jersey Trail Conference Ashokan Rail Trail (nynjtc.org/sites/default/files/NYNJTC_AshokanRailTrailMap_2019Oct.pdf)
Special considerations: This is a paved wheelchair-accessible route. Fishing is permitted on the reservoir with a DEP Access Permit. *Note:* While there are some benches to rest on, there is no shade along this walk.

FINDING THE TRAILHEAD

There are two parking areas—Frying Pan (27 B West South Rd.) and Olivebridge Dam (NY 28A just west of NY 213).

Frying Pan: Take New York State Thruway exit 19 (Kingston). Take I-87 North and NY 212 West to Maverick Road in Woodstock. Keep right at the fork and follow signs for I-87 North/Albany; merge onto I-87 North. Go about 9.5 miles and take exit 20 for NY 32 toward Saugerties. Turn left onto NY 212 West/NY 32 North and continue to follow NY 212 West for 8.6 miles. Turn left onto NY 375 South/West Hurley Road. Drive 1 mile and turn right on Maverick Road. In 2 miles continue on NY 28 West. Drive to B West South (BWS) Road in Marbletown. After 8.3 miles make a sharp left on BWS Road. Parking is on the left.

Olivebridge Dam: Take New York State Thruway exit 19 (Kingston). Make a slight right onto NY 28 West and continue 3.4 miles. Turn left onto Waughkonk Road and then make an immediate right onto NY 28A West. Continue for 10.8 miles. The parking lot is on your right, just after the intersection with NY 213. Trailhead GPS: N41 94.853' / W74 18.144'

THE HIKE

The Ashokan Reservoir is one of six Catskills reservoirs that are part of a system that includes valve chambers, treatment facilities, and more than 127 miles of aqueducts and tunnels. Built in the early 1900s, the Ashokan Reservoir would deliver 600 million gallons of freshwater to New York City, doubling the existing supply at the time. Today it supplies about 40 percent of New York City's drinking water. The name "Ashokan" is based on the Native American word *sokan*, which means "to cross the creek."

A dividing weir separates the upper west and lower east basins of the Ashokan Reservoir.

Creating the reservoir came at a great cost that included the work of 3,000 men, a $20 million price tag, and the removal of local people from their homes. Four hamlets were permanently removed, and eight others were relocated to higher ground.

Engineers built 40 miles of highways and ten new bridges, excavated 2.5 million cubic yards of earth and rock, used 1.2 million barrels of cement to build adjacent facilities, and planted 1.5 million new trees to prevent erosion. Although the Ashokan's water began flowing downstate in 1917, bad feelings still linger over the ways New York City's water needs were met.

Because the water must remain pristine, boating and logging are by permit only; you cannot bring a gas-powered vehicle onto the water, and swimming is prohibited. In fact, the water from these Catskills reservoirs is so clean that it only needs minimal treatment before reaching consumers.

The rail trail runs along the north side of the Ashokan Reservoir (see box); the promenade trail is located on the reservoir's south side. The promenade, a paved, flat, carless

ASHOKAN RAIL TRAIL (ART)
The rail trail, located on the north side of the Ashokan Reservoir, is an 11.5-mile gravel trail that runs between Basin Road in West Hurley and NY 28A in Boiceville. The trail, completed in 2019, is built on what had been the Ulster & Delaware (U&D) Railroad Corridor, which was abandoned in 1977. Volunteer trail stewards assist with the operation of the ART, which is made possible through a continuing partnership with the New York–New Jersey Trail Conference and the Woodstock Land Conservancy. The trail connects to the Ashokan Reservoir Promenade via Reservoir Road.

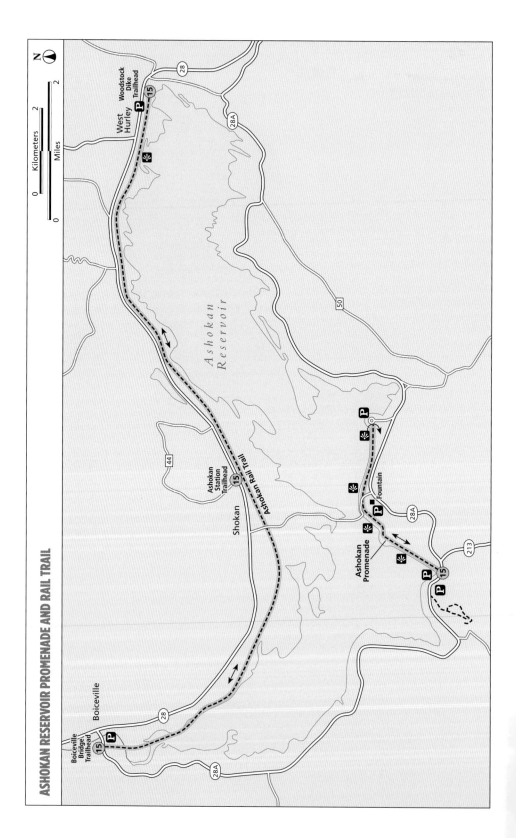

ASHOKAN RESERVOIR PROMENADE AND RAIL TRAIL

Ashokan Reservoir

Woodstock Dike Trailhead

West Hurley

Ashokan Station Trailhead

Shokan

Ashokan Rail Trail

Boiceville

Boiceville Bridge Trailhead

Ashokan Promenade

Fountain

28

28A

44

50

213

15

N

Kilometers

Miles

The fountain, surrounded by 5 acres of public land, makes it a great spot for a picnic.

route, follows the water's edge and offers a drop-dead-gorgeous backdrop of Catskills peaks that includes Ashokan High Point, Sugarloaf, Twin, Indian Head, Overlook, and the smaller peaks of Ticetonyk, Tonshi, and Little Tonshi Mountains. You may see bald eagles and deer as you make your way end to end (from one parking area to the other).

There are two off-trail features that might capture your interest. One is a 104–year-old monument to the Ashokan Reservoir project engineers, in particular chief architect J. Waldo Smith. The monument's stone tower was originally used to measure and survey the land. The other site is the Ashokan Fountain, originally used as an aerator, with valves to regulate water flow. It's surrounded by 5 acres of public land that make a great spot for a picnic.

MILES AND DIRECTIONS

0.0   Start from the Olivebridge Dam parking area. Cross over onto the promenade. (Crossing the dam is a one-lane bridge known locally as the "lemon squeeze." Originally two lanes, the bridge was narrowed after 9/11 to deter evildoers from harming the reservoir.)

1.0   Pass Reservoir Road on your left. Stay on the promenade. On your right is the Ashokan Fountain.

2.5   Arrive at the Frying Pan (east) parking lot. Turn around and head back.

5.0   Arrive back at the parking lot.

With the Catskill Mountains as backdrop, the paved trail beckons cyclists, walkers, runners, and roller bladers.

16 ASHOKAN QUARRY TRAIL

History and scenery meet on this new path through a stone quarry, with railroad remnants, old buildings, and a rise to an expansive view of the mountains.

County: Ulster
Start: In the parking area off NY 28A in Olivebridge, overlooking Ashokan Reservoir
Elevation gain: 167 feet
Distance: 2.0-mile lollipop
Difficulty: Easy
Hiking time: About 1.5 hours
Seasons: Year-round
Schedule: Open daily, dawn to dusk
Fees and permits: No fees or permits required
Trail contact: New York City Department of Environmental Protection; (718) 595-7000; www1.nyc.gov/site/dep/index.page
Canine compatibility: Dogs permitted on leash

Trail surface: Rock and gravel to start, becoming more gravel and dirt beyond the first 0.25 mile.
Land status: Protected by the Ashokan Watershed Stream Management Program, the New York City Department of Environmental Protection, and the Catskill Mountain Club
Nearest town: Olivebridge, New York
Other trail users: Trail runners; cross-country skiers (in season)
Maps: Catskill Mountain Club Ashokan Quarry Trail (catskillmountainclub.org/events/wp-content/uploads/2020/07/AQT-map-final.pdf)
Special considerations: Please be respectful of artifacts you encounter during your hike.

FINDING THE TRAILHEAD

From Kingston, take NY 28 West to Waughkonk Road in about 3.5 miles. Turn left on Waughkonk Road, and then turn right onto NY 28A. Continue on NY 28A for 11.2 miles, along the Ashokan Reservoir to Olivebridge, and watch for the signs for the Ashokan Quarry Trail. The parking area is on the left. Trailhead GPS: N41 56.123' / W74 13.733'

THE HIKE

When New York City needed to create a new water system in the early 1900s, it worked with the New York State Legislature to create the New York City Board of Water Supply—and that organization acquired land in Ulster County to build a reservoir. Critical to construction was the raw material required to contain 122.9 billion gallons of water in a massive reservoir, the largest and deepest built up to that time. That material came from the Yale Quarry, just west of Olivebridge Dam—and as of July 2020, you can take an easy trail through the quarry to see the remains of the operation that supplied the stone for the dam and reservoir.

Let's take a moment to revisit the origins of the Catskill region's rock. The mountains emerged as a result of the last two ice ages, 25,000 and 12,000 years ago, when glacial ice covered the entire region. As this ice melted, it formed lakes and streams that filled the gouges left behind by retreating glaciers. The bedrock below these water features came into being much longer ago in geologic time—during the Devonian period (about 400 million years ago)—but its top layer was largely sandstone and shale, much of which

The remains of the railroad loading bay still stands here.

traveled down mountain slopes with the meltwater and ended up on the bottoms of these streams and rivers. Today you can see this reddish clay in streambeds including Esopus Creek, one of the main watershed arteries that fill Ashokan Reservoir. The bedrock that remains within the mountains, however, provided exactly the kind of hard material required to build permanent structures like dams and reservoirs.

According to writer Luc Sante in the architectural publication *Places Journal* (doi .org/10.22269/201117a), the dam's construction required a kind of masonry used in ancient Greece by the Mycenaeans, known as "cyclopean" because it used very large blocks of stone. Such huge slabs could not be transported from far off without considerable expense and bother, but the Catskills themselves could provide plenty of stone from beneath its mountain surfaces. The Yale Quarry served up these massive chunks of sedimentary bedrock, which were dropped into concrete beds for formation into individual 83-foot sections of rock and cement. Each section was positioned by laborers in the 252-foot-high, 4,650-foot-long dam wall, their size allowing the dam to expand and contract with the weather to avoid any failure of the gigantic structure. "The whole undertaking would require the excavation of around two million cubic yards of dirt and 400,000 cubic yards of rock," Sante wrote. "It would call for 1,100,000 barrels of cement for 900,000 cubic yards of masonry; the embankments alone would require 7 million cubic yards of material."

Such an undertaking required more workers than the total populations of the towns that would be upended and submerged by the reservoir, so a camp sprang up to accommodate the 6,000 workers who arrived from the New York City area to complete the project—most of them immigrants from Italy, Poland, and the Slavic countries, as well as

Black workers, according to a 1909 article in the *New York Times*. Soon the camp became a village, complete with schools, churches, and its own police force. While some of these workers dug the reservoir and built the dam, others worked in the 1,200-foot-long Yale Quarry, cutting slabs from the rock walls and building a railroad to transport the stone from the quarry to the jobsite. A stone-crushing plant within the quarry could pulverize more than 70 cubic yards of stone in an hour, using gravity to load this stone into the railroad cars. When ten cars were filled, a coal-powered locomotive pulled them to the jobsite, a 15-minute trip at a cautious speed of 3 miles per hour.

More than 426,000 cubic yards of stone for the dam and the reservoir's intake chambers came from this quarry, and some material produced here served as armoring on the dikes around the reservoir to keep erosion to a minimum. The grueling work finally came to an end in June 1915, when the reservoir made water available to New York City for the first time.

The new Ashokan Quarry Trail, completed by the volunteers of the Catskill Mountain Club and opened in July 2020, takes you past the quarry's high walls to remnants of the railcar loading area, and then up about 150 feet in elevation to a particularly fine view of some of the Catskills' high peaks. On the way, you can see a stand of mountain laurel—particularly impressive in June, when it reaches full bloom—and a vernal pool at the base of the quarry wall.

At the top of the rock wall, hikers can see the Burroughs Range and other mountains.
Facing page: The new trail is well maintained and easy to follow.

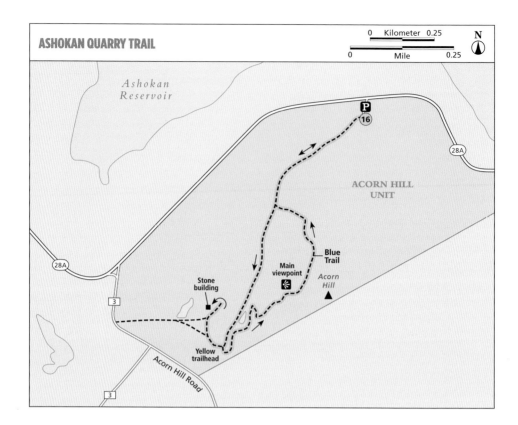

MILES AND DIRECTIONS

0.0 Start from the parking area trailhead. There is only one trail, leading southwest from here.

0.3 A small stone building here held explosives during the quarry's active years. In a moment, the blue-blazed trail goes left. Continue straight.

0.5 Pass a pond to the left at the base of the rock wall. In a moment, there's an interpretive sign about the quarry.

0.6 Take the yellow-blazed side trail to your right to remnants of the railroad.

0.8 The big man-made stone walls here represent the last of the railroad that hauled rock out of the quarry. When you are done here, return to the main trail and continue to where the signs point left. Go left, following the blue trail markers. The trail begins to slope upward. When it becomes open rock, watch the markers for a black arrow on a blue diamond. Go right, and continue to the top of the next rise.

1.1 Reach the unobstructed view you came to see. The Burroughs Range, North Dome, and Mount Tremper can all be seen from viewpoints along this stretch.

1.7 You have descended from the slight rise and are back at the main trail. Turn right to return to the parking area.

2.0 Arrive back at the trailhead.

17 ASHOKAN HIGH POINT

A great mix of easy and challenging terrain on an iconic Catskills peak, leading to some great views.

County: Ulster
Start: Peekamoose Road (CR 42), Kanape Brook Trailhead parking
Elevation gain: 1,963 feet
Distance: 7.4 miles out and back if you don't take the loop; 9.2 miles round-trip if you do
Difficulty: Easy to moderate
Hiking time: 4 to 5 hours round-trip, depending on whether you include the loop
Seasons: Year-round
Schedule: Open daily; camping areas available
Fees and permits: No fees or permits required
Trail contact: DEC Region 3 New Paltz Office; (845) 256-3076; email: r3forestry@dec.ny.gov

Canine compatibility: Dogs permitted on leash
Trail surface: Roots, rocks, hard-packed dirt, gravel
Land status: New York State Department of Environmental Conservation
Nearest town: Woodstock, New York
Other trail users: Campers; snowshoers (in season)
Maps: Mountain Hiking Ashokan High Point (mountain-hiking.com/ ashokan-high-point-loop/); New York–New Jersey Trail Conference Trail Map 143
Special considerations: This spot is popular with day hikers, but luckily the parking lot has recently been expanded.

FINDING THE TRAILHEAD

Take the New York State Thruway to exit 20 (Saugerties) and turn left out of the Thruway entrance road. Take a right onto NY 212 toward Woodstock and drive 8.5 miles west. Turn left onto NY 375 South and drive 3 miles to the road's end. Take a right onto NY 28 and continue approximately 9.7 miles to Boiceville. Turn left onto NY 28A (just as you enter Boiceville) and drive approximately 3 miles. Take a right onto CR 42 (Peekamoose Road) and go up the road about 3.5 miles. The parking lot is on the right. Trailhead GPS: N41 56.139' / W74 19.692'

Beavers have spent a good amount of time damming up this small pond.

Kanape Brook burbles alongside the trail, which starts out mellow but grows sharply steeper.

Eastern red-spotted newts scamper on the trail. Cute they may be, but these orange fellas secrete poisonous toxins.

THE HIKE

While Ashokan High Point, aka High Point, is not one of the highest peaks in the Catskills, it makes a towering appearance as it rises high above the Esopus Valley. Its profile—level summit and symmetrical sides—make it a local landmark.

At the beginning of the trail leading to High Point, you walk along Kanape Brook. The brook is named for John Canape, one of the first European settlers in the area. The Lenni Lenape and Esopus Indians had been hunting and fishing in this region for years, but in the 1760s European settlers began purchasing Catskill land. You'll pass bluestone dry walls (not mortared) and other remnants of farms long gone.

Much of the High Point Trail is surrounded on either side by thick stands of mountain laurel. There are also more than twenty tree species, including Norway spruce, maple, white pine, and oak, thriving on the mountainside—and lots of rocks. Local volunteers have put in place a set of rock "stairs" to help as the climb grows much steeper.

Just before the summit is a rock ledge viewpoint. Trees have overtaken the view, but in leaf-off season you can see Mohonk, Skytop, and the Shawangunk Ridge.

Sunk into the rock at the summit, you'll find three heavy bolts that were once anchors for an observation tower. There are also remnants of a plane wreck nearby. To find it, follow the trail past the summit; you may need to bushwhack your way through, as it's not frequently traveled. (As we attempted to find the wreck, a small bear crossed in front of us. We decided to head back down—we didn't want to find ourselves between this bear and its mother.) There are some open fields, as well, and lots of sweet and delicious blueberries if you're there in season.

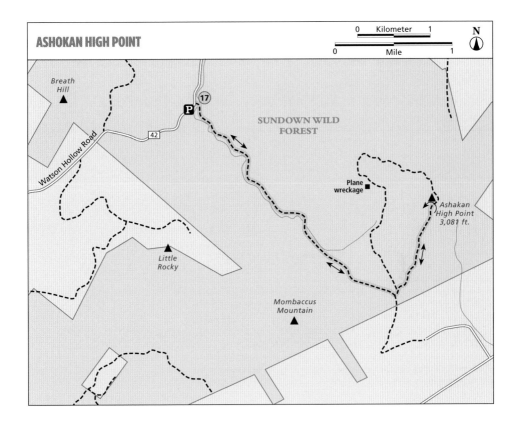

0   Kilometer   1

N

0   Mile   1

Breath Hill

SUNDOWN WILD FOREST

42

Watson Hollow Road

Plane wreckage

Ashakan High Point 3,081 ft.

Little Rocky

Mombaccus Mountain

MILES AND DIRECTIONS

0.0 Start from the parking area on Peekamoose Road. Signs direct you to the trailhead across the road, about 250 feet. You will immediately come to a footbridge over a brook and a red trail marker. After a few hundred feet, sign in at the register. The trail runs along Kanape Brook.

1.7 Cross the brook on a small wooden walkway and start veering away from the water. Keep following the red-blazed trail.

2.8 Turn left and keep following the red trail markers.

2.9 What looks like a social trail on the left—but is likely just overgrown from disuse— goes to the northern trail. (**Option:** This trail adds about 1.7 miles if you're doing a lollipop.) Take the right fork to head directly to Ashokan High Point summit. The trail is steep.

3.3 Bear left at red markers.

3.6 There's a viewpoint off to the right.

3.69 You've reached Ashokan High Point summit. Retrace your steps to the parking lot. (**Option:** Continue on the longer western route about 1.7 miles to the junction with the trail back to the parking lot.)

7.4 Arrive back at the trailhead.

18 WALLKILL VALLEY RAIL TRAIL: NEW PALTZ TO ROSENDALE

A walk in the woods to an ingeniously repurposed train trestle and fabulous valley views.

County: Ulster
Start: Parking/fishing access area on Springtown Road at Cereus Way, outside New Paltz
Elevation gain: 242 feet
Distance: 3.4-mile shuttle (6.8 miles out and back)
Difficulty: Easy
Hiking time: About 2.5 hours as a shuttle
Seasons: Year-round
Schedule: Open daily, dawn to dusk
Fees and permits: No fees or permits required
Trail contact: Wallkill Valley Rail Trail Association, PO Box 1048, New Paltz 12561; wvrta.org
Canine compatibility: Dogs permitted on leash

Trail surface: Packed dirt, some mowed grass areas
Land status: Wallkill Valley Rail Trail Association
Nearest town: New Paltz and Rosendale, New York
Other trail users: Cyclists, equestrians, joggers, trail runners; cross-country skiers (in season)
Maps: NatGeo TOPO! Map (USGS): Rosendale, NY; NatGeo Trails Illustrated Map #750: Shawangunk Mountains; trail map available online at wvrta.org/enjoying-the-trail/map/
Special considerations: In-town sections of this trail can be heavily used on weekends. Consider a weekday hike instead.

FINDING THE TRAILHEAD

From New Paltz, take NY 299 West to Springtown Road; turn right on Springtown. Continue 4.1 miles to the parking area for fishing access to the Wallkill River (GPS: N41 48.133' / W74 05.116'). Park here and cross Springtown Road on foot to Cereus Way, where you have access to the Wallkill Valley Rail Trail.

For the shuttle, park your destination car in the lot on Binnewater Drive in Rosendale, just off NY 213. From New Paltz, drive north on Springtown Road to the junction with NY 213 in Rosendale. Turn left on NY 213 (Main Street) and watch for the turn onto CR 7/Binnewater Drive. Turn right on Binnewater and continue to the parking area, on your left (GPS: N41 50.893' / W74 05.272'). Trailhead GPS: N41 48.183' / W74 05.215'

THE HIKE

If you saw the words "rail trail" in the title of this hike and assumed this would be just another flat, dog-walking and jogging path for local residents, let me assure you that this section of the Wallkill Valley Rail Trail is something truly special. This path leads through farmland, pastures, and unusual rock formations until it reaches the Rosendale Trestle, a 940-foot-long, 150-foot-high railroad bridge that has been reimagined for foot and bicycle traffic.

The Wallkill Valley Rail Trail sprang from the inspiration of a group of volunteers who, back in 1983, saw an opportunity to turn the disused railroad bed into an asset the entire region could enjoy. They persevered for years to wrangle the many different companies, organizations, and agencies involved until they finally had the necessary permissions to begin clearing the tracks and converting the corridor to a natural environment. The trail opened in 1991, but its development has continued in the ensuing

See where the railroad broke through rock formations to form a straightaway.

decades as the Wallkill Valley Rail Trail Association carries out its plans to lengthen, expand, and improve its resources.

The opening of the refurbished Rosendale Trestle represents one of the association's most laudable accomplishments. Originally built in 1872, the trestle stood as the highest span bridge in the United States, and it served until the Wallkill Valley Railroad took its last run in 1977. Turning the bridge into a destination for hikers, runners, cyclists, and sightseers required a fundraising campaign to raise the $1.5 million required, but the association partnered with the Wallkill Valley Land Trust, and their efforts succeeded. The trestle reopened in 2013 and instantly was a hit with both residents and visitors.

The trestle crosses Rondout Creek in the town of Rosendale and provides an unprecedented view of the creek's own forest-covered valley to the west, with an equally impressive view of downtown Rosendale in the opposite direction. At one end, Joppenbergh Mountain juts into the continuing trail; the other end skims the tops of tulip trees for a serendipitous display of blooms if you happen to visit in mid-May.

The Rosendale Trestle provides the grand finale for an entirely satisfying hike that begins on Springtown Road in New Paltz. We chose this particular starting place because of its easy parking and trail access, and because we wanted to explore the newest section of the rail trail. The section described here is part of the recent 11.5-mile extension of the trail from New Paltz through the town of Ulster, bringing the trail's total length to 22 miles.

Whether you hike this section or a longer one, keep in mind that there's much more to see on this rail trail than the trestle. You'll cross a section of the venerable Mohonk Preserve via the Lime Kiln Trail, just south of the mountain road. A trail up to Joppenbergh Mountain starts behind Main Street in Rosendale, and then a cave-like limestone mine opening emits blasts of frigid air on even the hottest days. In between you'll share the trail with chipmunks, squirrels, rabbits, and white-tailed deer, and you're almost certain to see blue

The Rosendale Trestle has become a favorite spot for people throughout the Walkill Valley.

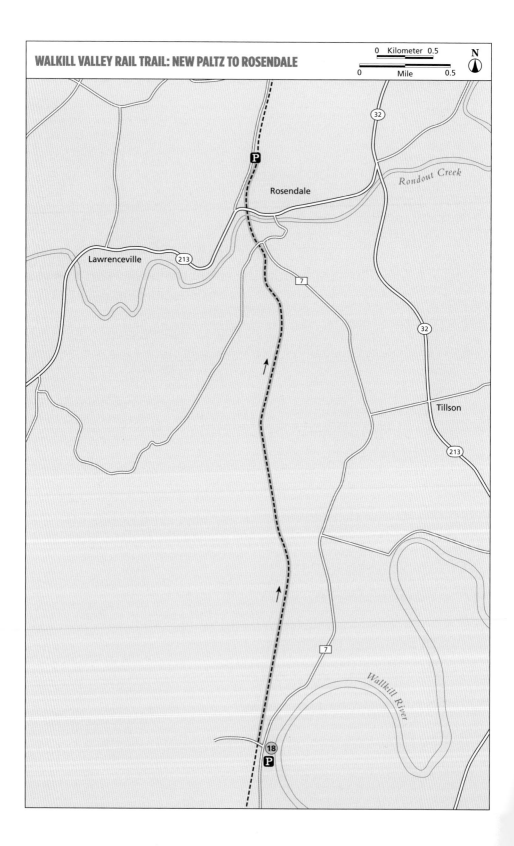

0   Kilometer 0.5

0   Mile   0.5

N

Rondout Creek

32

P

Rosendale

Lawrenceville   213

7

32

Tillson

213

7

Wallkill River

18

P

A recent renovation of the Rosendale Trestle produced a pedestrian passage over the Walkill River.

jays scouting for food and northern cardinals swooping from tree to tree. The trail may be flat, but its attractions are many—so put away your smartphone and keep your eyes open.

MILES AND DIRECTIONS

0.0   Start from the parking area, cross Springtown Road, and proceed to your right to Cereus Way. The gravel rail trail appears to your right.

0.3   Eddie Lane crosses the trail. Continue straight.

0.5   A farm lane crosses the trail. There's a nice view to your left of the nearest ridges of the Shawangunks. Watch for occasional remnants of the railroad tracks embedded in the ground.

1.1   A long private driveway crosses the trail.

1.2   In this rock face you can see the drill cuts made by workers who conducted the blasting operations to clear the way for track construction.

1.3   A bridge crosses a stream and a road here.

1.4   In the clearing to your left you'll see the Rail Trail Cafe (open on weekends in season). There's a bike rental shop here as well.

2.0   A neighborhood access trail enters from the right. You'll see a lot of these in the next mile or so. As the trail begins to follow a stream on your left, you're adjacent to the lands of Mohonk Preserve.

2.6   Here's an interpretive sign for the Grant's Ledges Pocket Park.

2.9   Cross the road in the crosswalk. In a moment you've reached the Rosendale Trestle Bridge. If it's May, look right to see if the massive tulip tree is in bloom.

3.1   The trestle bridge ends. You can see a trail to your right, but it's not the official trail to Joppenbergh Mountain. Do not take this trail up—it has many loose gravel sections and is not safe. The trail to the top starts and returns in the parking area behind Main Street in the town of Rosendale. Continue straight to stay on the rail trail.

3.3   Take this turn to the left to the destination parking area.

3.4   Arrive at your shuttle vehicle.

NORTHWESTERN CATSKILLS

This area of Catskill Park boasts the highest peak, Slide Mountain, at 4,180 feet. Back in 1892, Arnold Henry Guyot, a Swiss-born professor of geography and geology at Princeton University, proved that Slide Mountain was the highest in the Catskills.

In one of his many essays about Slide Mountain, environmental conservationist John Burroughs described it this way: "You see, amid the group of mountains, one that looks like the back and shoulders of a gigantic horse. The horse has got his head down grazing; the shoulders are high, and the descent from them down his neck very steep; if he were to lift up his head, one sees that it would be carried far above all other peaks, and that the noble beast might gaze straight to his peers in the Adirondacks or the White Mountains. But the lowered head never comes up; some spell or enchantment keeps it down there amid the mighty herd; and the high round shoulders and the smooth strong back of the steed are alone visible."

All this interest in Slide Mountain proved helpful in the creation of the New York State Forest Preserve.

Post–Revolutionary War, with little attention paid to preserving the land and the state needing money, attracting industry became the main goal. The state sold off large swaths of land in the Adirondacks and Catskills to private individuals and companies. In 1792, Alexander Macomb was able to purchase 3.6 million acres. (Pre-Revolution, in 1706, Johannes Hardenbergh purchased 2 million Catskill acres from the Esopus tribe, but that's a different tale, told earlier in this book.) Most of the new landowners were loggers and railroad companies, tanners, and paper manufacturers—all interested in timber. For the next seventy-five years, they depleted the land of resources, lessening its value. The companies stopped paying their taxes and pulled up stakes, and the "worthless" land reverted to the state.

In addition, settlements and farms began to encroach on the forests. Hunters took advantage of the plentiful game and wildlife. Railroads brought people to newly built hotels and spas. The wilderness was fading away.

By the mid-1800s people became interested in conservation. Writers and thinkers like Burroughs, James Fenimore Cooper, Ralph Waldo Emerson, Walt Whitman, and Henry David Thoreau and painters like Thomas Cole, who founded the Hudson River School with its tradition

The view from Pratt Rock's higher ledges provides a look at the entire region. (Hike 21)

of landscape painting, all brought attention to the importance of the natural world.

It took until 1885 for New York State to establish the forest preserve—two, in fact: one for the Adirondacks and one for the Catskills. Seven years later, after Guyot had surveyed the land, the state spent $250 to build a trail up Slide Mountain. It was the first hiking trail paid for by the public. That path was just the beginning of all the footpaths and horse and snowmobile trails that make up this great recreational network.

A quick, steep climb leads to an outstanding view of the Schoharie Valley; bring a picnic lunch and linger at the top.

County: Schoharie
Start: Trailhead in the parking area on Mill Valley Road in Fulton
Elevation gain: 485 feet
Distance: 1.8 miles out and back
Difficulty: Moderate
Hiking time: About 1 hour
Seasons: Spring through early fall
Schedule: Open daily, dawn to dusk
Fees and permits: No fees or permits required
Trail contact: NYSDEC Division of Lands & Forests, 625 Broadway, 5th Floor, Albany 12233; (518) 473-9518; dec.ny.gov/lands/80993.html

Canine compatibility: Dogs permitted on leash
Trail surface: Dirt path
Land status: Recently acquired by the New York State Department of Environmental Conservation
Nearest town: Fulton, New York
Other trail users: Joggers, trail runners
Maps: AllTrails Vroman's Nose Loop (alltrails.com/trail/us/new-york/vromans-nose-loop-trail)
Special considerations: Be prepared for an elevation change of nearly 500 feet in 0.6 mile.

FINDING THE TRAILHEAD

From Schenectady, take I-88 west to exit 22 (Cobleskill/Middleburgh/NY 7). Turn left at the end of the exit ramp and follow NY 145 south into Middleburgh. At the junction with NY 30, turn right (southwest) and follow NY 30 to Mill Valley Road (you'll see the unmistakable cliffs of Vroman's Nose in front of you). Continue west for 0.6 mile on Mill Valley Road, and watch for the parking area on your left (south). Trailhead GPS: N42 35.680' / W74 21.495'

THE HIKE

If you're willing to tough out the 0.7-mile climb to the top of this imposing cliff, your efforts will be well rewarded. From the summit of Vroman's Nose in the town of Fulton, you'll enjoy a 270-degree view of the pastoral Schoharie Valley, from the town of Middleburgh to the northeast to thousands of acres of fertile, cultivated farmland to the north, east, and south—all part of the Schoharie River's alluvial floodplain at the northern end of the Catskill Mountains.

This limestone, shale, and Hamilton Group sandstone peak, carved out by glaciers as much as 50,000 years ago, underwent a series of transformations as the massive ice sheets melted and deposited sediments. Over thousands of years the glacial activity isolated this bedrock peak and shaped its striking profile—and when Adam Vroman arrived here in 1713 and established the area's first farm, his name quickly became associated with the landform. Only the most devoted historians will recall Vroman's Land Massacre of 1780—an incident between European-descendant settlers and the area's Iroquois Indians—but members of the Vroman family survived the assault and have continued to live in this valley ever since.

Several trails lead to the summit, but the directions here take you up the easiest path. While you can follow a different path back from the summit to create a loop, the other paths are significantly steeper and require some careful hiking during the descent. I

The trail up Vroman's Nose leads to a series of high ledges.

recommend returning the way you came, back down the aqua-blazed trail. If you choose to use the blue- or yellow-blazed trail to return to the parking area, you may find yourself hanging onto trees to slow your progress down the slope. A red-blazed trail leads straight down the western wall of the Nose—follow this one at your own risk.

A word about the aqua blazes: You will see this unusual color on several hikes described in this book, and with good reason. These trails are all part of the Long Path, a footpath from Altamont in the Albany area all the way to the George Washington Bridge in Fort

Vroman's Nose is easy to identify as you approach.

Lee, New Jersey. Originally a project of the Mohawk Valley Hiking Club back in 1929, this 347-mile trail crosses the Shawangunk and Catskill Mountains, winding through salt marshes at its southern end and climbing to 4,000 feet in the Catskills' boreal forests. It's only recently that the "parakeet aqua" blaze color has been used from one end of the trail to the other, but wherever you see this shade, you'll know you're on the Long Path. Watch for it in Mine Kill State Park as well.

MILES AND DIRECTIONS

0.0 Start at the only trail leading into the woods from the parking area, through the two metal gates. Follow this trail to the point at which two trails diverge, and then follow the aqua blazes up the hill.

0.3 Bear right (west) on the well-worn path. In about 50 feet, the yellow-blazed trail goes left (southeast). Go right.

0.5 Reach the trail registry. You're nearly at the top of the rise.

0.6 Stop to catch your breath and admire your first great view of the area. Limestone and sandstone outcroppings serve as steps as you climb.

0.7 You're at the top. Congratulations! Continue along the summit of the Nose as the view becomes even broader.

0.8 Arrive at the tip of the Nose. The town slightly to the left (northeast) is Middle-burgh; the plowed fields below bear a wide range of vegetables, changing with the seasons—from asparagus in spring to pumpkins, squash, carrots, and parsnips in fall. The orchards you see provide some of New York State's famous apples and other fruits.

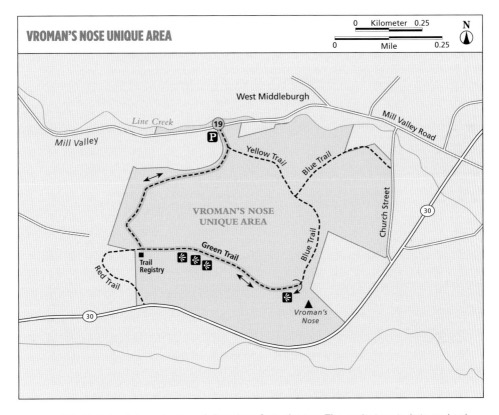

VROMAN'S NOSE UNIQUE AREA

0   Kilometer   0.25

0   Mile   0.25

N

West Middleburgh

Line Creek

Mill Valley

Mill Valley Road

Yellow Trail

Blue Trail

VROMAN'S NOSE
UNIQUE AREA

Church Street

30

Green Trail

Blue Trail

Trail
Registry

Red Trail

30

Vroman's
Nose

0.9   Trails lead down in several directions from the top. The easiest route is to go back the way you came up, especially if you're hiking in winter or early spring, when the path may be snow-covered or wet and slippery.

1.8   Arrive back at the parking area.

At the top, the view provides plenty of reward for the burst of effort required to get here.

20 MINE KILL STATE PARK

A wide, mellow creek, a placid reservoir, and a young forest make this hilly trail the perfect place to see the seasons change in the northern foothills of Catskill Park. On an alternate trail, three waterfalls chase one another down the walls of a narrow gorge.

County: Schoharie
Start: The main trailhead is at the entrance to the parking area at the end of Mine Kill State Park Road. For the shorter waterfall hike, find the trailhead at the park's south entrance off NY 30.
Elevation gain: 403 feet
Distance: 1.9-mile loop for the main trail; additional 0.8 mile out and back from the south entrance for the waterfall hike
Difficulty: Moderate
Hiking time: About 1.5 hours
Seasons: Spring through fall
Schedule: The park is open Memorial Day to Labor Day, 7:30 a.m. to dusk. Winter hours are 7:30 a.m. to 4:30 p.m.
Fees and permits: Fee charged per vehicle in season

Trail contact: Mine Kill State Park, 161 Mine Kill State Park, North Blenheim 12131; (518) 827-6111; parks.ny.gov/parks/minekill/details.aspx
Canine compatibility: Dogs permitted on leash
Trail surface: Dirt path with wooden stairs
Land status: New York State Park
Nearest town: North Blenheim, New York
Other trail users: Joggers, trail runners, cross-country skiers, mountain bikers, snowmobilers
Maps: Mine Kill State Park (parks.ny.gov/documents/parks/MineKillTrailMap.pdf)
Special considerations: Bow hunting is permitted in fall; wear blaze orange if you hike in November and December. Be sure to leave the park by dusk.

FINDING THE TRAILHEAD

From Middleburgh, take NY 30 South for 17 miles. The park entrance is on NY 30, past the New York Power Authority complex. Enter the park and drive east on Mine Kill State Park Road until it ends at the parking area near the reservoir boat launch. The trailhead is at the entrance to the parking area. Trailhead GPS: N42 26.414' / W74 27.243'

Note: If you just want to hike to the waterfalls, return to NY 30 and drive north for 1.2 miles to the park's south entrance. Trailhead GPS (waterfalls): N42 25.638' / W74 28.290'

THE HIKE

While the main attractions at Mine Kill State Park relate to water—fishing, boating, and swimming in the park's Olympic-size pool—8 miles of trails give hikers the opportunity to enjoy the park's succession forest and breeze-tossed meadows on foot. The hike described here brings you to one of the park's best scenic overlooks, from which you can view the Blenheim-Gilboa Pumped Storage Power Project, tucked below Brown Mountain to the east. The power project generates as many as 1 million kilowatts of electricity during peak demand, using Schoharie Creek to create the electricity and returning the creek's water to two reservoirs—the one you see at the park; the other 2,000 feet up at the top of Brown Mountain. Learn more about this unusual power source at nypa.gov/communities/visitors-centers/blenheim-gilboa-visitors-center.

Lower Mine Kill Falls flows into a grotto-like gorge.

This entire area is an excellent example of a process environmental scientists call "forest succession." As recently as a few decades ago, these woods were farmers' cultivated fields. Plants, shrubs, and trees returned to the land through seeds blown on the wind. Other seeds were sown by unsuspecting animals, birds, and insects as they carried food or deposited their waste in the area. The result is thriving woodland that will be a thick forest in a few more decades—part of the process of natural succession.

The hike takes you up and down the hilly terrain so typical of the Catskill foothills, providing enough challenge to hold your interest while leading you along ridges and down pleasantly gentle slopes. Parts of this route are labeled with interpretive signs to help you identify the trees, plants, and flowers you see, while also providing information about the changing nature of the park's wildlands. You may leave with the ability to tell the difference between eastern white pine and eastern hemlock, or with a new understanding of power generation and its role in this area's growth and development.

If you enjoy waterfalls as much as we do, you can extend your hike here with an out-and-back walk along the Long Path, a 347.4-mile walking trail from Altamont (near Albany) in New York State to the George Washington Bridge in Fort Lee, New Jersey. The Long Path joins many shorter trails in this region, and its distinctive aqua/turquoise blazes make it easy to follow. The path extends southwest from the orange-blazed trail described below, providing an additional scenic hike that culminates in views of three waterfalls: Lower Mine Kill, which drops through a notch at the top of a magnificent hidden gorge; Middle Mine Kill, a connecting chute that leads your eye to a glimpse of the best of the three falls still far below you; and the 80-foot Upper Mine Kill Falls, a dramatic cascade in a limestone alcove. You can see cement structures left over from the dam at the top of the falls, but these remnants don't detract from the impressive power of the falling cascade you see here. In high-water seasons, check the gorge for additional temporary cascades and curtain falls sprinkling (or pouring) down its sedimentary walls.

MILES AND DIRECTIONS

0.0 Start at the trailhead and follow the red-blazed trail. Take the mowed path through the meadow and cross the road.

0.1 Proceed up the hill to the scenic overlook.

0.2 From the scenic overlook you can see the Blenheim-Gilboa Pumped Storage Power Project, including the dam that creates this reservoir from Schoharie Creek. There are picnic tables and benches here, as well as restrooms. When you are ready, continue south on the red-blazed path you followed to the viewpoint. (Another red-blazed trail goes south from the restrooms. Both lead in the right direction and connect with the orange-blazed trail to the south.)

0.3 Turn right (west) on the orange-blazed trail, and walk downhill to a nice view of the surrounding hills and treetops.

0.4 At the intersection, bear right on the combined red- and orange-blazed trails.

0.6 The orange-blazed trail splits and goes toward some buildings to the right. Continue straight (west).

0.9 The orange-blazed trail makes a sharp left and briefly joins the aqua-blazed trail (the Long Path). Here you can turn left on the Long Path to view the waterfalls, adding 0.8 mile out and back to your hike. (See the additional miles and directions below.) Otherwise, continue on the orange-blazed trail. From here, much of the path is downhill. Cross a meadow with tall grasses and wildflowers then reenter the forest.

1.3 Cross a runoff stream on rocks.

1.5 Bear right on the orange-blazed trail. This is where Schoharie Creek and the Blenheim-Gilboa Reservoir join, to your right.

1.6 Bear right (east) on the yellow-blazed trail. (**Option:** Rejoin the red-blazed trail and return to the overlook.) To complete this loop, follow the yellow-blazed trail, which is a bit more hilly and rugged.

1.8 Cross the road and return to the trailhead at the parking area.

1.9 Arrive back at the parking lot.

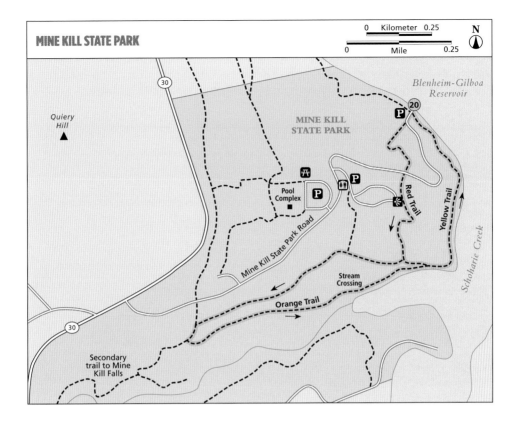

0   Kilometer 0.25

0   Mile   0.25

N

Blenheim-Gilboa Reservoir

30

20

P

MINE KILL
STATE PARK

*Quiery
Hill*

▲

P

Pool
Complex
■

P

Red Trail

Yellow Trail

Schoharie Creek

Mine Kill State Park Road

Stream
Crossing

Orange Trail

30

Secondary
trail to Mine
Kill Falls

MILES AND DIRECTIONS FOR WATERFALL HIKE

0.0   Leave the orange-blazed trail at 0.9 mile on the main trail and follow the aqua-blazed Long Path.

0.1   A signpost directs you left and down to the Lower Falls. Leave the Long Path and go left.

0.2   The trail emerges from the woods at the plunge pool for the Lower Falls. There's plenty of open gravel here even in high-water season, so you can walk around freely. Seeing the whole falls takes some maneuvering, as it has worn away the gorge wall behind it and is now nestled back into the rock. When you're ready, head back up the trail to the Long Path and turn right.

0.4   Reach a series of landings connected by stairs, with great views of the falls. At the bottom of the stairs, the long chute falls (Middle Mine Kill Falls) comes into view. Walk down the aisle created by two fences and reach a gravel path with many wooden steps. This quickly becomes a wooden staircase. Upper Mine Kill Falls is on your left as you start down. When you're ready to return to the trail, go back up the stairs to the Long Path and return the way you came.

0.8   Arrive back at the orange-blazed trail. Pass the first junction with the orange-blazed trail and take the second one to your right to complete the loop. Follow the directions above, beginning at 0.9 mile.

21 PRATT ROCK TRAIL

When a man makes a monument to himself, attention must be paid. Luckily, he put it a short walk from some gorgeous Catskill views.

County: Greene
Start: Parking area on NY 23 just outside Prattsville
Elevation gain: 454 feet
Distance: 0.7 mile out and back, with an option to continue for another 2.4 miles round-trip through Pratt Rock Park
Difficulty: Moderate
Hiking time: About 1 hour
Seasons: Spring through fall
Schedule: Open daily during daylight hours
Fees and permits: No fees or permits required
Trail contact: Zadock Pratt Museum, 14540 Main St., Prattsville 12468;
(518) 299-3395; zadockprattmuseum.org
Canine compatibility: Dogs permitted on leash
Trail surface: Woodland floor with some flat rocks
Land status: Pratt Rock Park, Town of Prattsville
Nearest town: Prattsville, New York
Other trail users: Primarily hikers
Maps: AllTrails Pratt Rock Trail (alltrails.com/trail/us/new-york/pratt-rock-trail)
Special considerations: The trails are not marked, so pay close attention to find the side trail up to the carvings.

FINDING THE TRAILHEAD

From the town of Catskill, take NY 23 west for 36 miles. Turn left at the junction with NY 23A and continue for 0.5 mile to Pratt Rock Park. Trailhead GPS: N42 18.584' / W74 25.341'

THE HIKE

Gather 'round for the tale of Zadock Pratt Jr., a businessman and statesman whose accomplishments ranked among the highest in the Catskills at the time—a list of achievements that have been memorialized on the mountain that bears his name. Called "the Mount Rushmore of the East" by local residents (Rushmore architect Gutzon Borglum need not worry that his reputation will be challenged), the symbols carved in stone represent specific moments in Pratt's life: a bust of his own likeness, a memorial to his son, George, a horse, a tree, the family coat of arms, Pratt's tannery, a wreath that contains his two children's names, and a disembodied arm raising a hammer.

If this description hasn't made the history of Pratt's Rock any clearer, let me start at the beginning. Zadock Pratt grew up in the Catskill region from his birth in 1790 and joined the New York militia in 1819. He distinguished himself in military service, becoming colonel of the 116th Regiment in 1822 and holding this rank until his discharge in 1826.

Once he returned to the Catskills, Pratt built a tannery—a processing plant where animal skins are turned into leather—and grew it to become the largest in the world. Soon he founded a town to support his workforce of about 2,000 people, naming it Prattsville. The town thrived as the tannery business expanded, bringing Pratt visibility as a savvy businessman and natural leader. When he ran for the US House of Representatives in 1836, he won the election; he won a second term in 1842—and in 1845 he became the first congressman to propose a transcontinental railroad. He ran for governor of New

Hikers can see the craftsmanship in the carvings when they arrive on this ledge.

York in 1848 and lost, but he retained his political capital, serving as a delegate to the 1852 Democratic National Convention.

Pratt maintained a number of other projects even as he served in Congress. In 1843 he established the Prattsville Bank, which offered its own currency on par with the US dollar—but the currency didn't catch on, and he closed the bank nine years later. He moved on to finance several smaller tanneries in the Catskills, and even partnered with future

Pratt Rock's carvings can be seen from the ground.

railroad magnate Jay Gould to establish a tannery in Pennsylvania. In 1860, he decided to retire; he lived another eleven years.

It may (or may not) surprise you to learn that the story of how Pratt's Rock came to bear a series of symbols illustrating Zadock Pratt's life is a bit cloudy. Surely the execution of such a publicly visible project must have been obvious to many townspeople, and we can assume that it generated quite a bit of gossip and curiosity at the time. Even so, three different stories about the project circulate to this day. The first involves Pratt meeting stonecutter Andrew Pearse as he passed through town on foot. Pearse requested lodging for the night, but instead of simply giving him money or food, the story goes, Pratt—who believed that all people should work for their keep—engaged him to carve a horse on a gray sandstone rock face on his property. As he saw Pearse's handiwork, the project grew; Pratt had the stonecutter create a monument to himself and, later, to his son, George, who died fighting in the Civil War's Second Battle of Manassas in 1862.

Other accounts change the story a bit: Pratt asked the stonecutter to carve a bust of himself in a large rock at an intersection of two dirt roads, one leading to Windham and the other to Lexington. The stonecutter began carving, but a man named John Brandow arrived at the intersection. Brandow informed Pearse and Pratt that the rock was on his land, and "he did not want Pratt's face on it to haunt him as he passed. Brandow did not like Pratt," an account repeated in the *Stamford Mirror-Recorder* in 1958 tells us. Pratt then directed the stonecutter to move to a high rock face on Pratt's own land to recommence his work, and the rest has become history. Yet a third account relates that Pratt went looking for a stonecutter to create the images he had in mind and selected one of the most skilled in the area—though the name of that artist is unknown.

The Zadock Pratt Museum suggests that none of these stories is true, as evidenced by the inconsistencies in style and technique from one carving to the next. Instead, the museum holds that a series of stonecutters worked on the wall over a twenty-eight-year period, naming little-known artists including Pearse, John Fair, Charles Kissock, E. Brevier, and I. H. Vermilyea as possible participants. Kissock—who was born in 1859, long after this project started, and who had a stonecutting business in a nearby town—may have come in at the end to do some cleanup of others' carvings, perhaps even after Pratt's death.

Regardless of how this wall of carvings came to be, Pratt donated 20 acres of land to the town of Prattsville in 1843, including the rock face we now know as Pratt's Rock. The public could picnic here, take walks, and scramble up to the top to enjoy sweeping views of the Catskill Mountains. Over time, they also had the opportunity to follow paths to the carvings and to benches cut out of the rock, where they could rest and take in the peaceful scene below.

Another facet of this tale seems meant to deliberately mislead visitors: the location of Pratt's own grave. Zadock Pratt originally planned to be interred at Pratt's Rock in a grotto carved for this purpose, but the grotto—which you can see when you reach the wall of carvings—proved to be unstable, with water leaking into its depths, making burial here impossible. Today a tombstone appears to mark Zadock's grave at the base of the mountain as you begin your hike. He is not buried here, however—his remains

Zadock Pratt commissioned a stonecutter to create this memorial to the son he lost in the Civil War.

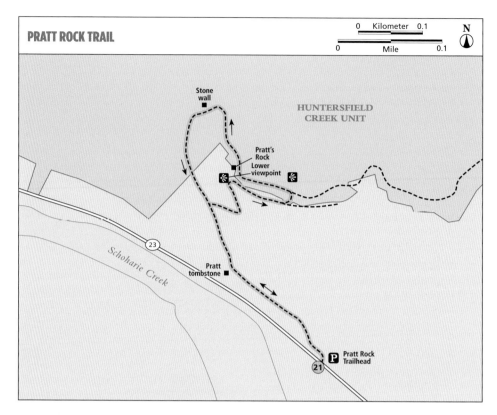

rest in the town's cemetery. Even in death, Zadock Pratt made certain he would have the last word about how he would be remembered, linking his epitaph with the wall that chronicles his life.

MILES AND DIRECTIONS

0.0   Start at the parking area. The trail proceeds northwest, past the kiosk to your left as you face the mountain. In about 250 feet, pass Zadock Pratt's tombstone.

0.1   A trail goes sharply to the right. This is the trail to the actual carvings. Turn right and follow the zigzagging path upward. In about 100 feet, you can see most of the carvings through a break in the foliage. This is the best place to view the whole sculpture. Continue up another 100 feet or so to a wide ledge, where you can walk the length of the carvings and see them up close. The view of the surrounding landscape is quite nice from here as well. When you're ready, continue up the trail.

0.2   The trail comes out at a higher ledge. You can walk along here to the east to enjoy a number of viewpoints from which you can see a wide area of the Catskill Mountains. When you're ready, walk back toward the trail to the carvings—but this time, continue straight ahead on the gentler path.

0.4   Reach a stone wall with a cleft in the middle. Pass through the cleft and continue down the trail.

0.7   Arrive back at the parking area.

With a little imagination, you can see how farmers might have lived on this former estate. The multiuse trail makes for a great kid-friendly hike, mountain bike, or horseback ride.

County: Ulster
Start: Matyas Road parking lot
Elevation gain: 869 feet
Distance: 6.4 miles (if you wander all three trails)
Difficulty: Easy to moderate
Hiking time: About 3 hours
Seasons: Year-round
Schedule: Open daily. Camping areas available.
Fees and permits: No fees required; permit needed for motorized assistance vehicles
Trail contact: DEC Region 3 New Paltz Office; (845) 256-3076; email: r3forestry@dec.ny.gov
Canine compatibility: Dogs permitted on leash
Trail surface: Packed earth, carpet of leaves and pine needles

Land status: New York State Department of Environmental Conservation
Nearest town: Phoenicia, New York
Other trail users: Snowshoers, cross-country skiers (in season); mountain bikers, horseback riders
Maps: Shandaken Wild Forest (dec .ny.gov/docs/lands_forests_pdf/ recmapswf.pdf); New York–New Jersey Trail Conference Trail Map 142
Special considerations: There's an ATV access route for those needing motorized assistance. Contact the local DEC office for a permit. Not every part of this trail system is ADA compliant. ***Note:*** Locals might tell you that you need a four-wheel-drive vehicle to get to this parking area and trailhead, but we had no trouble driving here in a two-wheel-drive vehicle on a misty day in July 2021.

FINDING THE TRAILHEAD

From the New York State Thruway take exit 19 (Kingston). Turn right onto NY 28 West and drive for about 28 miles. You'll pass through the hamlet of Big Indian before turning right onto Matyas Road. Look for DEC signs for Rochester Hollow. Trailhead GPS: N42 11.803' / W74 45.168'

THE HIKE

Col. William B. Rochester, for whom this trail was named, was the eldest son of Col. Nathaniel Rochester, founder of the city of Rochester, New York (4 hours to the west). William made a name for himself in the War of 1812 as an aide-de-camp to Gen. George McClure. After the war he practiced law, was elected to the New York State Assembly and then the US Congress. He was appointed a judge on the Eighth Circuit Court and resigned in 1826 to run for governor of New York, only to lose to DeWitt Clinton.

Rochester purchased small farms to create Rose Hill Estate, the parcel that is now the trail site. The trail was an old carriage road. There are three ways to enjoy the trail: The Colonel Rochester Trail, blue markers, is 4.4 miles out and back. Off that trail is the Burroughs Memorial Forest Trail, yellow markers, a 1.2-mile loop on its own (or 0.8 mile from the red trail until it connects again to the blue trail); and the Eignor Farm Trail, red markers, 1.35 miles connecting one part of the blue trail to the other.

Above: A lovely path for a contemplative walk.
Below: A small monument, one of many in the Catskills, to conservationist John Burroughs.

JOHN BURROUGHS FOREST

MEMORIAL TO THE BELOVED NATURALIST, AUTHOR, AMERICAN
OF SLABSIDES AND THE WORLD. REFORESTED BY HIS NEIGHBORS
THE BOYS OF THE RAYMOND RIORDON SCHOOL AND TO BE GIVEN
THEIR PERPETUAL JOYOUS CARE UNDER THE DIRECTION OF
NEW YORK STATE CONSERVATION COMMISSION

Remnants of the small farmsteads that dotted this former estate.

The trail is located in the Shandaken Wild Forest and parallels a tributary of Birch Creek north for 1.75 miles before making a sharp turn west for the remaining 0.45 mile. The trail is somewhat narrow and well delineated by low vegetation, ferns, and old hemlock trees. It's soft underfoot and a comfortable walk that's relatively flat for the first mile. After that it gets steeper, but only slightly.

As you walk along, you'll come upon the remains of stone buildings that once belonged to farming families. Take a few minutes to wander along the long, low stone fences and the remnants of a large carriage garage. It's a great spot to let kids climb, explore, and imagine how life might have played out for a farmer on this tough land.

You'll come upon a lean-to, which is dedicated to James Smith, a Catskills trail supervisor. The clean and tidy wooden shelter faces a large firepit and the woods beyond. Camping is allowed in the lean-to. There's also a clean privy nearby.

The John Burroughs Memorial is set off under the tree canopy. Erected in 1921, the year of Burroughs's death, the memorial honors the naturalist and author whose love of the Catskills helped inspire the conservation movement.

The trails are well marked for paths used by hikers, cyclists, and wheelchair users.

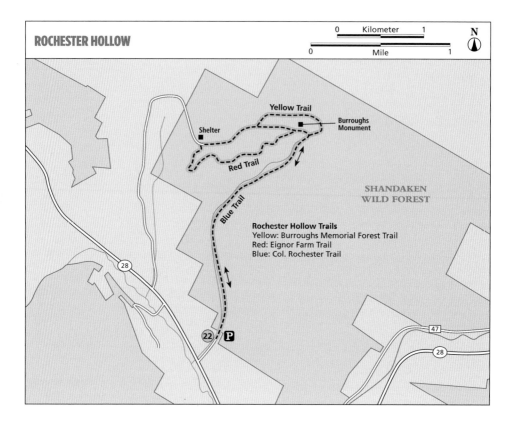

0   Kilometer   1

0   Mile   1

N

Yellow Trail

Shelter

Burroughs
Monument

Red Trail

Blue Trail

SHANDAKEN
WILD FOREST

Rochester Hollow Trails
Yellow: Burroughs Memorial Forest Trail
Red: Eignor Farm Trail
Blue: Col. Rochester Trail

28

22   P

47

28

MILES AND DIRECTIONS

0.0 Start from the parking lot and head up the hill on the blue-blazed trail. Sign in at the registry before continuing. Follow the blue markers.

0.2 On your left is a marker denoting camping. Continue following the blue-blazed trail up a gradual incline.

1.2 Reach a gateway of stone pillars, one on each side of the trail.

1.75 Junction with the Burroughs Memorial Trail (yellow). The Burroughs monument is to your left in about 0.1 mile. (**Option:** If you bear right, you'll be on the yellow-blazed Burroughs Memorial Trail. The trail loops counterclockwise. You can follow this trail for 1.2 miles to end up back at this junction then return to the parking area via the blue-blazed Colonel Rochester Trail.) Or, instead of walking in a loop, remain on the yellow Burroughs Memorial Trail until you've gone 1.25 miles to meet up with the western leg of the blue trail.

2.9 End of the ATV-access route. The Rochester Hollow lean-to is just up a small hill on the right. After visiting (or camping), head back down to the trail. Turn right to continue on the blue-blazed trail. The trail blaze becomes blue. Follow to complete the loop.

4.7 Crossroad; the red-blazed trail ends. Turn right to pick up the blue-blazed trail to return to the parking area.

6.4 Arrive back at the parking area.

23 GIANT LEDGE/ PANTHER MOUNTAIN

This trail delivers a big bang for your buck: amazing 75-mile views from the top of this at-times challenging trail.

County: Ulster
Start: Oliverea Road (aka Fire House Road); trailhead is across the street from the marked parking area on CR 47 in Shandaken, New York.
Elevation gain: 2,035 feet
Distance: 3.75 miles out and back to Giant Ledge; 6.4 miles out and back to Panther Mountain
Difficulty: Difficult
Hiking time: About 2 hours round-trip to Giant Ledge; about 4 hours round-trip if you go all the way to Panther Mountain
Seasons: Year-round
Schedule: Open daily. Camping areas available.
Fees and permits: No fees or permits required
Trail contact: DEC Region 3 New Paltz Office; (845) 256-3000; email: r3admin@dec.ny.gov; (518) 408-5850, or dial 9-1-1

Canine compatibility: Dogs permitted on leash
Trail surface: Dirt; large, loose rocks; tree roots
Land status: New York State Department of Environmental Conservation
Nearest town: Phoenicia, New York
Other trail users: Campers
Maps: CalTopo (https://caltopo .com/m/R6JT); AllTrails Giant Ledge and Panther Mountain (alltrails.com/ explore/trail/us/new-york/giant -ledge-and-panther-mountain-trail ?mobileMap=false&ref=sidebar-static -map); New York–New Jersey Trail Conference Trail Map 142
Special considerations: Wear sturdy hiking shoes with good ankle support. Bring crampons for winter or early-spring hiking.

FINDING THE TRAILHEAD

From the New York Thruway (I-87) headed north from Poughkeepsie/New Paltz, take exit 19 for the Kingston-Rhinecliff Bridge. Head west (away from the bridge) on NY 28 and continue for another 30 miles. At Big Indian, turn left onto CR 47 (Oliverea Road; sometimes marked as Fire House Road). In 7.4 miles there's a sharp turn to the right that heads up a large hill. Parking for Giant Ledge is on the right, just before that sharp turn. A wooden sign on the shoulder marks the parking lot. Trailhead GPS: N42 02.639' / W74 40.24'

Note: There is only room for about 15 cars, and the lot is crowded on weekends. Parking on the road near that sharp turn can be dangerous.

THE HIKE

Most mountains are created by shifting tectonic plates, but in the mid-1990s, scientists posited that Panther Mountain was actually created by a meteor impact.

The discovery was made by geologist Dr. Yngvar Isachsen, who saw, via satellite imagery, a circular feature surrounding the mountain formed by Esopus Creek and a tributary called Woodland Creek. Isachsen studied the area and, based on certain evidence—fractured streambed joints, small iron-rich glassy spheres, and shocked quartz—theorized that the mountain began its life some 400 million years ago when a meteor slammed into what was then a subtropical sea. Over the ensuing years, post-impact sediment and

Worth the climb: a panoramic view of the Catskills from one of the five ledges. JEFF GRAF

broken rock eventually filled in the crater. Not all scientists agree with this theory, but the evidence is compelling. Today, 3,720-foot Panther Mountain is a great way to start a Catskills adventure—and everyone knows it. If you can do this hike during the week instead of a weekend, you have a better shot at experiencing some awe-inspiring views without a crowd.

The hike can be steep at times, but whether you're pushing uphill or leisurely strolling on flat ground, watch your footing. The trail is crossed by tree roots and littered with rocks, some tall enough that you will have to pull yourself over as you climb. It is as though you're walking up a dry creek bed (which you likely are), and you'll cross many small active creeks along the trail. Thankfully, in many spots, trail volunteers have purposefully lined up rocks diagonally across the trail to divert water.

While you're busy watching your footing, you've still got to look up to find the trail. Although well marked with the standard Catskill circular colored metal markers—and you're only going from yellow to blue—all the rocks can make it difficult to figure out the correct path. But stay the course and you'll be rewarded with areas for breathtaking views known as Giant Ledge, literally outcroppings (there are five of them) large enough to hold ten to fifteen people. If you're lucky enough to be there on a slow day, you may have a slab of rock to yourself and a view that extends 75 to 80 miles.

Not far from the ledge areas are two campsites tucked back into the trees. They are pretty bare bones: DEC has removed some amenities, as things have gotten pretty rowdy and some less-careful campers have left trash.

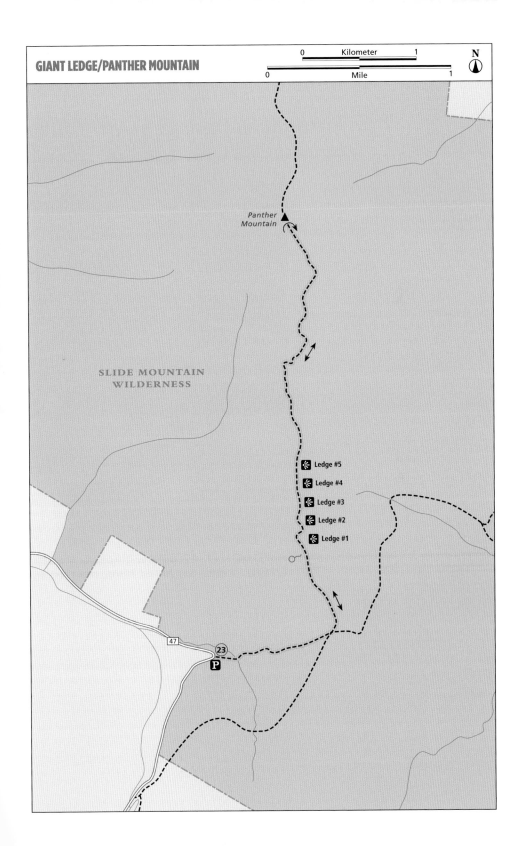

0   Kilometer   1

0   Mile   1

N

Panther
Mountain

SLIDE MOUNTAIN
WILDERNESS

Ledge #5

Ledge #4

Ledge #3

Ledge #2

Ledge #1

47

23

P

If you continue hiking—and it's mostly steep—for another half hour or so, you'll reach the summit, but you'd better whip out an altimeter, because there is no marker when you actually hit the highest point.

MILES AND DIRECTIONS

0.0 Start at the trailhead, which is across the street from the parking area. A few yards ahead, sign in at the register. Follow the yellow trail marker.

0.8 The blue-blazed trail begins. The sign reads "Giant Ledge .8 miles. Panther Mt 2.6 miles." Stay on the blue-blazed trail. You'll be going up about 1,000 feet to Giant Ledge.

1.3 On your left is a sign for a spring. If you need water and have a purifier, you can grab some.

1.5 The climb is fairly steep until, on your right, is your first ledge. (On your left is a campsite marker; a large camping area is a just a little ways into the woods.) Enjoy the view. In the distance is Devil's Path, and closer in across the valley are Cornell and Wittenberg, Terrace Mountain, Cross Mountain, and others toward Phoenicia.

1.55 Giant Ledge #2

1.6 There's a camping area off on a side trail on your left, about 150 feet off the trail.

1.67 Giant Ledge #3

1.76 Giant Ledge #4

With so much water cascading down and criss-crossing the trails, it can feel like you're hiking up a streambed. Watch your footing. STACEY FREED

1.87 Giant Ledge #5. (*Option:* You can turn around here and head back down.) For this hike, continue on to Panther Mountain.

2.1 The trail dips about 200 feet in the saddle between Giant Ledge and Panther Mountain. Follow the blue markers for about 1.0 mile (730 feet up) to the top of Panther.

2.7 You've reached the Department of Environmental Conservation's 3,500-foot elevation sign.

3.2 Hooray! It's the top of Panther Mountain, 3,720 feet. There's a nice flat but small rock from which you can take in the view. There's no summit marker. Head back down, following the blue-blazed trail to the yellow-blazed trail. Keep your eyes open for this junction. It's easy to let your enthusiasm carry you along the blue-blazed trail and past the turnoff.

6.4 Arrive back at the trailhead.

24 SLIDE MOUNTAIN

Because you've *got* to climb the highest point in the Catskills, but— *shhhh*—don't tell anyone it's not as difficult as they might think.

County: Ulster
Start: Oliverea Road DEC parking area
Elevation gain: 1,794 feet
Distance: 6.8-mile loop (can be done out and back in 5.6 miles)
Difficulty: Moderate to strenuous
Hiking time: About 4.5 hours
Seasons: Year-round
Schedule: Open daily. Camping areas available.
Fees and permits: No fees or permits required
Trail contact: DEC Region 3 New Paltz Office; (845) 256-3076; email: r3forestry@dec.ny.gov
Canine compatibility: Dogs permitted on leash

Trail surface: Roots, rocks, streambed
Land status: New York State Department of Environmental Conservation
Nearest town: Woodstock, New York
Other trail users: Snowshoers (in season); campers
Maps: AllTrails Slide Mountain (alltrails.com/explore/trail/us/new-york/slide-mountain-trail?mobileMap=false&ref=sidebar-static-map); New York–New Jersey Trail Conference Trail Map 143
Special considerations: The Neversink River may create very wet conditions, possibly impassable, at the start of this hike.

FINDING THE TRAILHEAD

Take New York State Thruway exit 19 (Kingston). Turn right onto NY 28 and go approximately 30.4 miles west. Take a left onto CR 47 (Oliverea Road) at Big Indian and continue for 9.4 miles south. The DEC parking lot is on the left side of the road, just after the Burroughs Historic Site sign. Trailhead GPS: N42 00.856' / W74 42.769'

THE HIKE

At 4,180 feet, Slide Mountain is the park's highest peak and the number-one high peak on the Catskill 3500 Club's list, which shows thirty-three Catskill mountains over 3,500 feet in elevation. The club defines the high peaks this way: "There must be at least a 250-foot drop between the peak and any other peak on the list, or the peak must be at least a half-mile away from any other peak on the list."

The club was founded in 1962 to encourage people to hike the Catskills' highest peaks. To be a member you have to climb the thirty-three listed mountains *and* complete four designated winter climbs between December 21 and March 21. You fill out a tally sheet, which can be downloaded from the club's website (catskill-3500-club.org), and pay a nominal fee to the club to show you've accomplished the task. The club also runs scheduled group hikes. A few of the hikes are trailless, so going with experienced hikers is encouraged.

While Slide is the highest peak, getting to the summit from the parking lot can really be done in about 90 minutes. Yet it will be challenging, as you steadily climb nearly 1,800 feet over 2.8 miles. You'll cross two streams, which, after rain or snowmelt, may contain 2 feet of rushing water. In between you'll wander along old carriage roads that are flat and wide. Just before the summit there's a ledge from which you have a great view of

Early morning at the top of the highest Catskills peak.

John Burroughs slept here—at least according to this monument.

Woodland Valley, Giant Ledge and Panther Mountain, Wittenberg Mountain, and the Indian Head Mountain Range. At the summit there's not much fanfare, but there is a square, flat block on the path to let you know you've arrived. Years ago, there was a fire tower here.

Travel a bit past the summit marker to the flat-topped area of layered rock about 10 feet high that's a memorial to John Burroughs. On its top is etched graffiti dating back to the 1880s—some things never change. Walk around the rock to find a plaque in memory of naturalist and writer John Burroughs. Several tall, striated rocks butt together here, with a small cave between them. The plaque says that Burroughs "introduced Slide Mountain to the world. He made many visits to this peak and slept several nights beneath this rock."

MILES AND DIRECTIONS

0.0   Start at the parking area and sign in at the register. (*Note:* It is quite possible that you will have to cross a relatively high stream at the entry to the trail.) Begin the trail, following yellow markers up a short rocky path.

0.5   Trail sign; turn right and continue following yellow markers.

0.8   Arrows direct you to turn left and begin heading up on the red-blazed trail.

1.3   Campsite marker on the right. Stay left, continuing on the red-blazed trail, which will get steeper.

1.5   Come to the 3,500-foot elevation marker. Celebrate, but keep climbing; the smell of pine will carry you along.

2.1   Reach a sign showing that Slide Mountain is only another 0.7 mile. Follow the red trail markers.

Top: Graffiti dating back to 1881, etched into the rock atop the Burroughs memorial. STACEY FREED
Bottom: The stone at the summit, where there used to be a fire tower. STACEY FREED

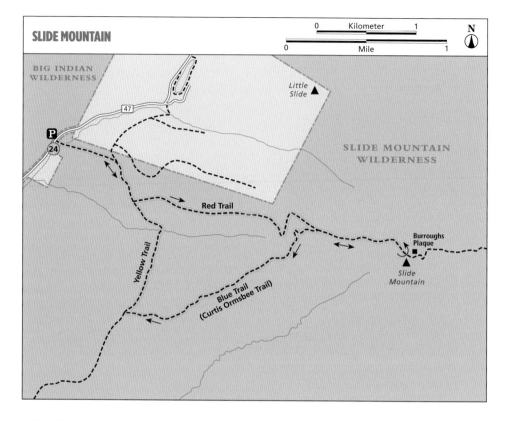

SLIDE MOUNTAIN

0 Kilometer 1

0 Mile 1

N

BIG INDIAN
WILDERNESS

Little
Slide

SLIDE MOUNTAIN
WILDERNESS

Red Trail

Burroughs
Plaque

Slide
Mountain

Yellow Trail

Blue Trail
(Curtis Ormsbee Trail)

2.8 You've reached the summit. A little farther on is a large boulder with a John Burroughs memorial plaque. (**Option:** Turn around and head back the way you came on the red-blazed trail.) For this hike description, return via the red-blazed trail for about 0.7 mile from the Burroughs memorial. Then turn left and follow the blue-blazed Curtis Ormsbee Trail back. This adds a little to the trip but makes the hike more interesting than going straight back down.

4.7 Reach a social trail and a view off to the left (best if leaf-off season). Stay right on the blue-blazed trail.

4.8 Pass a marked camping area with firepit off to the right. Stay on the blue-blazed trail as it travels down steeply over rocks.

5.3 There's a small campsite and firepit just off-trail to the left. Remain on the blue-blazed trail.

5.4 Arrive at a crossroad. Turn right onto the yellow-blazed trail. (If you make a left and a quick right, there's a campsite big enough for maybe four to five tents.)

6.0 Bridge across a creek. Stay on the yellow-blazed trail back to the parking lot.

6.8 Arrive back at the parking lot.

25 TABLE MOUNTAIN

Enjoy this one for the hiking itself and the surrounding forest scenery. It's a challenging hike to grab Number 8 on the list of Catskills 3,500-foot peaks.

County: Ulster
Start: Denning Road trailhead
Elevation gain: 1,709 feet
Distance: 7.8 miles out and back
Difficulty: Difficult
Hiking time: About 4 hours
Seasons: Year-round
Schedule: Open daily. Camping areas available.
Fees and permits: No fees or permits required
Trail contact: DEC Region 3 New Paltz Office; (845) 256-3000; email: r3admin@dec.ny.gov
Canine compatibility: Dogs permitted on leash
Trail surface: Roots, rocks, soil

Land status: New York State Department of Environmental Conservation
Nearest town: About 1 hour from Kingston or Phoenicia, New York
Other trail users: Snowshoers (in season); campers
Maps: AllTrails Peekamoose and Table Mountains (alltrails.com/explore/trail/us/new-york/peekamoose-and-table-mountains-trail); New York–New Jersey Trail Conference Trail Map 143
Special considerations: The creeks may run high and be difficult to cross. Use the bridges.

FINDING THE TRAILHEAD

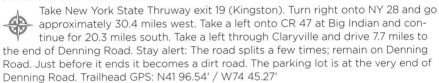

Take New York State Thruway exit 19 (Kingston). Turn right onto NY 28 and go approximately 30.4 miles west. Take a left onto CR 47 at Big Indian and continue for 20.3 miles south. Take a left through Claryville and drive 7.7 miles to the end of Denning Road. Stay alert: The road splits a few times; remain on Denning Road. Just before it ends it becomes a dirt road. The parking lot is at the very end of Denning Road. Trailhead GPS: N41 96.54' / W74 45.27'

THE HIKE

While a grand vista after a long hike is nice, sometimes you just want to hike for the solitude or the challenge of a tough climb, or for the smell of the air and the sound of the wind in the trees. Table Mountain offers that.

Table and Peekamoose are the southern Catskills' highest peaks, with Table only about 4 feet higher. If you've got the additional time, it's nice to experience both peaks. Peekamoose is a little less than 1.0 mile from Table's summit. Or you can hike the pair as a circuit with two vehicles, one parked at each end.

Starting from the Denning Road trailhead, the area feels as if you're really remote, but this is a popular hike among locals. Start on a flat carriage road through a forest of hemlock, beech, and yellow birch. In early spring the forest pops with violets, lilies, and purple trillium. A lot of the surrounding land is private, so stay on the carriage road. The route can get pretty wet as you cross and recross branches of the Neversink River and Creek.

Don't let the easy walk lull you; the trail soon gets steeper as you pick your way over rubble and rock. At one point you'll pass through giant striated rock slabs. Just before the summit there's a very steep 800- to 900-foot climb.

At the summit, a cairn and a tree seeming to stretch its branches in welcome.

Two of several bridges built by trail volunteers. Without them, the trail might be impassable.

White and light gray quartz pebbles line the summit's approach, stones that top only the southern Catskill high peaks. Per its name, the summit is flat. The true summit is at the western end; head east and the trail begins to dip. That's where you can catch a 120-degree north and west panorama, best seen in leaf-off season.

A natural log flume directs water down the mountain.

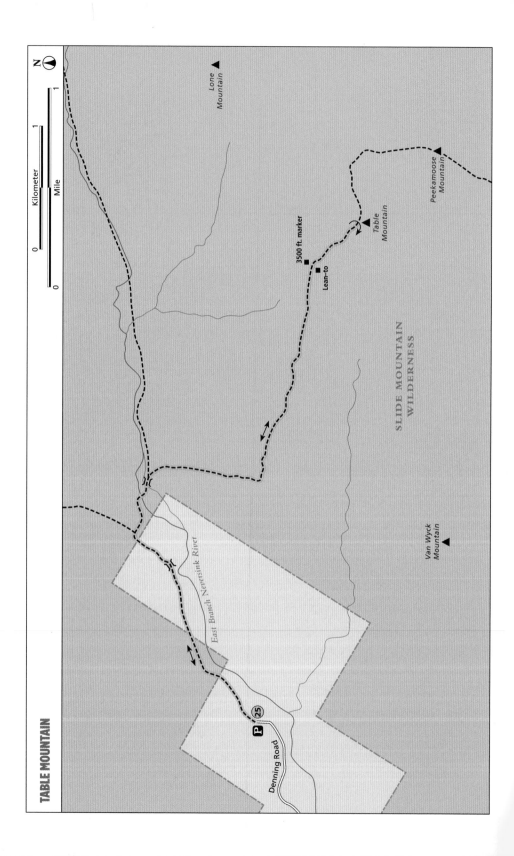

TABLE MOUNTAIN

N

0   1   Kilometer   1

0   Mile   1

Lone
Mountain

Peekamoose
Mountain

3500 ft. marker

Table
Mountain

Lean–to

SLIDE MOUNTAIN
WILDERNESS

Van Wyck
Mountain

East Branch Neversink River

P 25

Denning Road

Like many Catskills summits, there are no official markers letting you know you've arrived. If you know the correct elevation, there are apps you can use to let you know when you've reached the top. Otherwise, previous hikers have created a cairn to let others know they've reached the top. A cairn (from the Gaelic for "heap of stones") is a human-created stone stack. Cairns are universally understood by hikers and are found on trails around the world. Historically, they were used to mark safe routes, or as signposts for villages. In recent years, many organizations that protect natural areas, including the National Park Service, have come to consider these rock stacks a form of vandalism with unintended environmental consequences, hastening erosion and disrupting the flow of rivers. Also, if too many cairns line the way, hikers can get confused, thinking these piles of rocks are part of the trail-marker system.

After climbing Table Mountain, though, the 3-foot-high pile of stones (at the time of this writing)—standing alongside a gnarly tree that looks as if it just finished a pirouette—is a welcome sight, confirming your accomplishment.

MILES AND DIRECTIONS

0.0 Start at the Denning Road trailhead and sign the register. Follow signs for the yellow-marked Phoenicia–East Branch Trail.

1.1 Cross a small wooden bridge. (**FYI:** Some of the posted signs are from the nearby Frost Valley YMCA.)

1.3 Turn right onto the blue-blazed trail to Table and Peekamoose Mountains. (The trail to the left heads toward Slide Mountain.) The trail descends a bit at first.

1.5 Continue across a slightly rickety wooden bridge over the east branch of the Neversink River. Follow the blue marker on the other side.

1.7 Pass a firepit area on the right. Continue on the blue-blazed trail to yet another small wooden bridge (with only one handhold). Cross over and turn left on the other side. Continue following the blue trail markers.

1.8 Pass a camping area on the right. Stay straight on the blue-blazed trail.

3.2 Viewpoint off to the right. There's a big drop-off; watch your feet. Remain on the blue-blazed trail.

3.3 Sign for a spring on your left. (If there has not been a lot of rain, this spring may be dry.) Stay right for the blue-blazed trail.

3.4 Sign for a lean-to on the right. It's about 200 feet off the trail.

3.5 Reach the 3,500-foot marker.

3.7 Come to a small outcropping for a view (best in leaf-off season). Beware: There's a big drop-off here. Return to the trail and stay on the blue-blazed trail to the top; it will be steep.

3.9 Reach the summit. The trail is flat at the top; hence the name of the peak. Although there's no sign announcing the summit—other than a small cairn—pat yourself on the back; you've hiked to 3,849 feet. Enjoy a rest on the "table top" then retrace your steps to the parking area. (**Option:** Continue on about 0.85 mile through the col to the summit of Peekamoose Mountain.)

7.8 Arrive back at the trailhead.

26 RED HILL FIRE TOWER

A wonderful, short hike to one of the five remaining fire towers in the Catskills—and a spectacular panoramic view that takes in five states.

County: Ulster
Start: Dinch Road trailhead. (Dinch Road may also be known as Coons Road.)
Elevation gain: 1,020 feet
Distance: 2.8 miles out and back. (Starting at the new Denning Road trailhead at 2205 Denning Rd., Claryville, will make this a 4.0-mile out-and-back hike.)
Difficulty: Moderate
Hiking time: About 2 hours
Seasons: Year-round
Schedule: Open daily. Camping areas available.
Fees and permits: No fees or permits required
Trail contact: DEC Region 3 New Paltz Office; (845) 256-3076; email: r3forestry@dec.ny.gov

Canine compatibility: Dogs permitted on leash
Trail surface: Roots, rocks, dirt
Land status: New York State Department of Environmental Conservation
Nearest town: Liberty, New York
Other trail users: Campers; snowshoers, cross-country skiers (in season)
Maps: AllTrails Red Hill Fire Tower Trail (alltrails.com/explore/trail/us/new-york/red-hill-fire-tower-trail--2?mobileMap=false&ref=sidebar-static-map). The Catskills Visitor Center Map includes the new trailhead (catskillsvisitorcenter.org/place/red-hill-fire-tower/).

FINDING THE TRAILHEAD

From NY 17, take exit 105 in Monticello and follow NY 42 North to Grahamsville. Make a left onto NY 55 West. In Curry, turn right (north) onto Sullivan CR 19 toward Claryville. Proceed through Claryville and turn right onto Red Hill Road. Follow until you reach an intersection with Dinch Road (a dirt road, aka Coons Road). Make the sharp left onto Dinch Road and continue to the trailhead, on the right.

From NY 28, proceed to the hamlet of Big Indian, located west of Shandaken and east of Pine Hill. Turn south on CR 47 (Oliverea Road). Go approximately 21 miles, passing the Frost Valley YMCA, until you reach a three-way intersection. Make a left toward Claryville on Sullivan CR 19 and then right onto Red Hill Road. Continue until you reach an intersection with Dinch Road (a dirt road, aka Coons Road). Make the sharp left onto Dinch Road and follow to the trailhead, on the left. The parking is on the right; the trailhead is across the road. Dinch Road trailhead GPS: N41 92.293' / W74 50.57'

To the Denning Road parking area in Claryville: From Liberty, take NY 55 East/Neversink Road for 10.6 miles. Turn left on Claryville Road and drive for 5.3 miles. Continue onto Denning Road for 2.1 miles to the parking area, on your left. Denning Road trailhead GPS: N41 93.564' / W74 53.035'

THE HIKE

During the nineteenth and early twentieth centuries, fires ravaged New York State's forests. According to Martin Podskoch in *Fire Towers of the Catskills*, 643 fires destroyed 464,000 acres in the Adirondacks and Catskills in 1903. Five years later there were 605 fires in the Catskills, and more than 368,000 acres burned statewide.

The fire tower adds another 60 feet to your climb, and is well worth the added steps. Be prepared for a lot of wind at the top.

From the top of the fire tower, you'll get your fill of great views of the Catskills and five states.

This ranger station, built in 1931, is one of the oldest remaining observer's cabins in New York.

The old system of fire wardens—patrollers with the authority to order help to fight fires—wasn't enough. The staff was too small, and the state needed a way to prevent fires from getting out of control. In 1909 the Forest, Fish and Game Commission replaced the wardens with a more professional system of firefighters and had nine wooden fire lookout towers built. The firefighting system was based on a similar, successful system already in place in Maine.

Observers, soon known as "rangers," would sit in the enclosed "cab" at the top of the tower. There, they had a circular map on a table. The edge of the map was circled by a graduated ring (an azimuth ring) that helped them measure distance and direction. Atop the circle was a long bar called an alidade (a pointer) with 1-mile hash marks. The observer would sight along the alidade toward the smoke. The center of the map to the outside of the circle represented 15 miles. From this, the observer could pinpoint the location of a fire.

At one time there were 102 fire towers in operation. In 1912 the state was divided into five fire districts, and in 1916 the wooden towers began to be replaced with steel towers.

The system was in use until the 1980s, and in 1990 the fire tower at Red Hill was the last to be closed. Only five towers in Catskill Park still stand. (There's even a state-sponsored Catskills Fire Tower Challenge. Visit the DEC website, dec.ny.gov/lands/76620.html, for more information.)

The Red Hill fire tower was restored and reopened in July 2000. It is listed on the National Historic Lookout Register and has been nominated to the National Register of Historic Places. Today it is one of the most accessible of the Catskills' fire towers.

The hike from Dinch Road is relatively easy and ends at the summit, where in addition to the tower, there's an open field, picnic tables, and a small ranger station. A volunteer ranger is usually available (especially on weekends) to answer questions about the tower and the Catskills' history, and to assist you to the top of the fire tower.

Climb the 60-foot tower and you'll be rewarded with a 360-degree view. On a clear day you can see Massachusetts, Vermont, Connecticut, New Jersey, and Pennsylvania in the distance. Closer in, you get a spectacular view of the Catskill high peaks to the north and the Rondout Reservoir to the south.

On February 9, 2021, the New York State Department of Environmental Conservation opened a new parking lot, kiosk, and trail to improve access to the Red Hill Fire Tower and other trails in the Sundown Wild Forest.

The new parking lot, which can accommodate ten cars, is located at Denning Road. There, the newly established, blue-blazed trail traverses both city and state forest preserve lands. The projects were supported by the state's Environmental Protection Fund and partnerships with the New York City Department of Environmental Protection and the town of Denning.

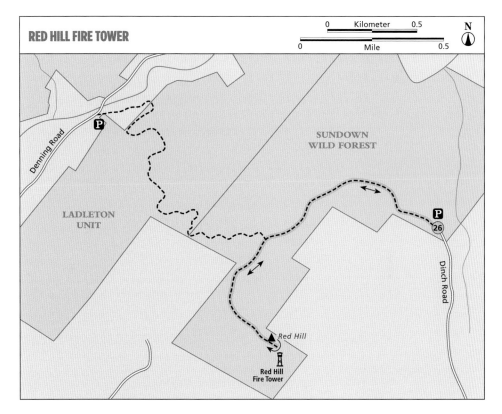

The trail winds upward through rocky outcroppings and hemlock–laden forests for 1.4 miles until it meets up with the existing blue-blazed trail, accessed from Dinch Road. The new trail makes the Red Hill Fire Tower visit a 4.0-mile out-and-back hike. (We chose the original entry to the trail instead of taking the newer entry solely because our NY–NJ Trail Conference map was printed in 2018 and did not have the new Denning Road trailhead marked.)

MILES AND DIRECTIONS

0.0 Start from the Dinch Road (Coons Road) trailhead. Follow the yellow trail markers and sign in at the register. Not far from the registry box, you'll cross a stream called Dinky Brook.

0.8 The trail switches to blue markers; stay left on the blue-blazed trail.

1.0 About 50 yards off to the right is a small waterfall and a spring with a pipe delivering cool, clear water. Just past here the trail turns left and heads uphill. But before you turn, check out the outcropping on your right. In leaf-off season, you'll get a nice view. Stay on the blue-blazed trail.

1.4 You've reached the top. Climb the fire tower steps for a panoramic view. Retrace your steps to the parking lot.

2.8 Arrive back at the parking lot.

Deep in the fragrant Willowemoc Wild Forest, you'll find a secluded wetland you can't see from the road, just begging for someone to explore it.

County: Sullivan
Start: Parking area on Beech Mountain Road, off Mongaup Road north of Anderson
Elevation gain: 78 feet
Distance: 2.2-mile lollipop
Difficulty: Easy
Hiking time: About 1.25 hours
Seasons: Spring through fall
Schedule: Open daily, dawn to dusk
Fees and permits: No fees or permits required
Trail contact: New York State Department of Environmental Conservation; (845) 256-3000; dec.ny.gov/lands/9146.html
Canine compatibility: Dogs permitted on leash

Trail surface: Rocky woodland floor, some mowed grass, some boardwalk; potential for mud
Land status: Willowemoc Wild Forest, protected by New York State Department of Environmental Conservation
Nearest town: Livingston Manor, New York
Other trail users: Equestrians; snowmobilers, snowshoers, and cross-country skiers (in season)
Maps: NYSDEC Willomewoc Wild Forest (dec.ny.gov/docs/lands_forests_pdf/recmapwwwf.pdf); New York–New Jersey Trail Conference Trail Map 144
Special considerations: This trail can be very muddy and slippery during wet seasons or after a rain.

FINDING THE TRAILHEAD

From NY 17 West, take exit 98 toward Parksville. Turn right onto Short Avenue and continue as this becomes Cooley Road. Keep left onto Lily Pond Road, and stay on Lily Pond as it becomes Old Lily Pond Road then Hunter Lake Road. Stay on Hunter Lake as it makes a slight left, and then turn left onto Willowemoc Road. Turn right onto Mongaup Road, and continue for 2.7 miles, where it becomes Beech Mountain Road. The parking area is on your left. Trailhead GPS: N41 57.077' / W74 42.411'

THE HIKE

Anglers know the Willowemoc River as one of the premier trout fishing waterways in the Catskills, but casual visitors may never come across the 40-plus miles of trails throughout the 14,870-acre Willowemoc Wild Forest. It's tucked away in the southwestern corner of Catskill Park, just inside the "Blue Line" that borders the park's protected woodlands. If you have hiked to the top of several of the peaks over 3,500 feet during your time in the park and you're looking for something not quite so challenging, this short hike provides a variety of peaceful habitats, wide views of water you can't see from the road, comparatively level terrain, and junctions with longer trails if you wish to explore further.

Most of Catskill Park contains forests at higher elevations than Willowemoc, with dense woodlands packed with a mix of conifers and leafy trees. This lowland forest

The trail takes its name from this picturesque pond.

features ponds, wetlands, and streams, and plenty of access to its interior along long-established woods roads that now serve as trails.

Long ago, the plentiful fish and game in these woods probably supported members of the Lenni Lenape tribe of the Algonquin nation, who developed the first trail through the area—known as the Sun Trail because it ran east to west from the Hudson River all the way to what is now the Binghamton area. A local Lenni Lenape group were known as the Willowemoc, lending the area their name. How long they may have lived in this area is difficult to pinpoint, but in 1706 a tribesman and sachem (wise man) named Naisinos sold about 2 million acres of land—essentially all of Sullivan, Ulster, and Delaware Counties—to Johannes Hardenbergh for 60 pounds, including the Willowemoc land. Hardenbergh and six partners received the patent (what we now call the title) for the land from the government of England in 1708, but many others challenged his claim to the desirable acreage, preventing it from being settled and developed until the American Revolution made it the property of the United States.

In 1811, when a second generation of owners had inherited the land, road builder Abel Sprague used the old Sun Trail as the route for the wider Hunter Road. It took him (and presumably a crew) four years to complete the road, but the new route supplied access to the area for people of industry—especially tanners, who required the forests' hemlock bark to treat animal hides with the tannin it contained. Tanneries sprang up in the surrounding towns, each of which cut down thousands of hemlock trees and peeled off their bark. Some of these denuded trunks were used as lumber, but as much as 95 percent of them "were left to rot in the woods," a Willowemoc Wild Forest management plan written in 1991 noted.

The thick foliage parts to make room for a quiet creek.

The razing of hemlocks opened the forest floor to hardwood trees that tolerated more sunlight, a development that attracted another industry: chemical manufacturing. Beech, birch, and maple trees contain natural chemicals that can be distilled for acids used in turning wool into cloth, using a process popular in Scotland at the time. Enterprising industrialists built acid-distilling factories and began cutting down the young trees to make methanol, acetate of lime, and charcoal, using massive quantities of local water

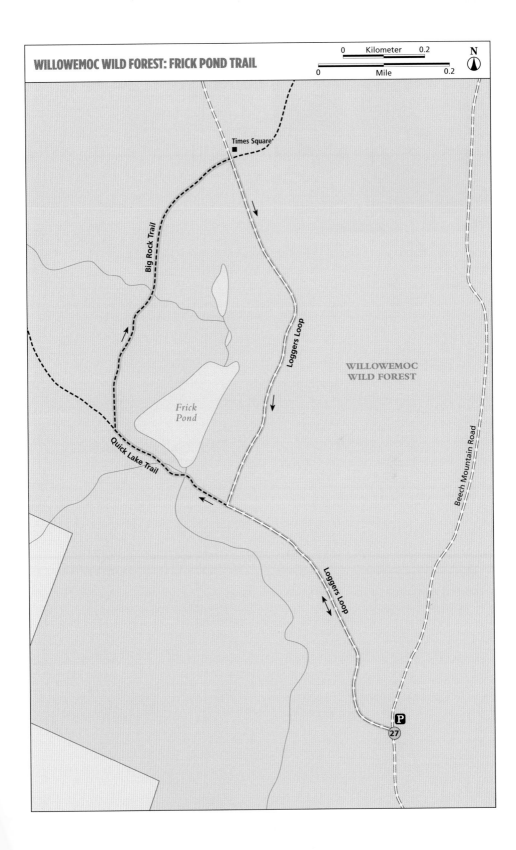

WILLOWEMOC WILD FOREST: FRICK POND TRAIL

0   Kilometer   0.2

0   Mile   0.2

N

Times Square

Big Rock Trail

Loggers Loop

WILLOWEMOC
WILD FOREST

*Frick
Pond*

Quick Lake Trail

Beech Mountain Road

Loggers Loop

P

27

Fans of native wildflowers can find blue-bead lily and other unusual plants blooming at Frick Pond.

to cool the machines that did this work. They found many markets for their products, from paint and varnish makers to photograph processors. Acid manufacturing produced a boom time in Sullivan County and throughout the southern Catskills until World War II, when clever scientists abroad developed synthetic chemicals that worked just as well as the ones processed from hardwoods. The industry collapsed, and the forests had the opportunity to restore themselves as the Catskills turned to tourism to produce income for the area's residents.

Meanwhile, New York State had begun to acquire the parcels to preserve Willowemoc Wild Forest as early as 1885, as landowners defaulted on their property taxes. The largest share of this land came from the daughter of Arthur Leighton, an acid factory magnate, who sold the land to the state in the early 1930s; more parcels were added in the 1960s and 1980s, including the former Beech Mountain Boy Scout Camp, which contained Frick Pond.

Today the scars of industrial use are all but invisible as you walk the forest trails. Successional hardwood forest has grown thick enough to form a canopy above hikers, blocking the sun and cooling the trails in summer and turning crimson and gold in the fall. Winter hiking can be especially delightful here, as many snowshoers and cross-country skiers can attest—but be sure to watch out for snowmobilers, as this forest is particularly popular among these folks.

MILES AND DIRECTIONS

- **0.0** Start at the trailhead, in the northwest corner of the parking area. You soon come to a trail register; be sure to sign in.

- **0.5** At the junction with Loggers Loop (yellow markers), turn left onto the Quick Lake Trail. You are following the orange markers.

- **0.7** Reach a bridge, where you have an unobstructed view of Frick Pond. Take your time and enjoy the view; it's the only place on the trail where you have this clear viewpoint. From here, pass through two areas dominated by hemlock trees and woodland filled with perching birds.

- **0.8** Turn right onto Big Rock Trail.

- **1.2** Come to an intersection known as Times Square, where four trails meet. Turn right and follow Loggers Loop (yellow markers) to close the loop.

- **1.7** Arrive back at the first junction. The bridge with the pond view is to the right; the trail register and the parking area are to the left. Go left. Don't forget to sign out at the register.

- **2.2** Arrive back at the trailhead.

SOUTHEASTERN CATSKILLS

One geologic wonder dominates Ulster County, in the southeastern corner of Catskill Park: the Shawangunk Ridge, a globally recognized destination for rock-climbing enthusiasts as well as more casual hikers. This wall of exposed bedrock, the dividing line between the Great Appalachian Valley to the east and the more mountainous region on its western side, contains a form of sedimentary rock so unique that geologists named it for the ridge itself. Shawangunk Conglomerate contains sandstone and white quartz, deposited on top of what is known as the Martinsburg Formation—the turbidite and gray shale layers beneath the conglomerate. This ridge arose about 420 million years ago, and eons of wind and weather have created the craggy, stratified strip of rock faces we see today.

Two magnificent nature preserves hide just behind the ridge's striking profile. Minnewaska State Park Preserve's rock promontories create the conditions for several particularly captivating waterfalls, as well as a sparkling sky lake surrounded by carriage roads—the century-old gift of wealthy residents of the area. Mohonk Preserve's 8,000-plus acres of forests, ponds, and cliffs are open to visitors through the graces of the Smiley family, who had the good sense to create a trust to preserve this magnificent property for the generations to come.

When you have frolicked among the Gunks to your heart's content, head down into the Great Appalachian Valley to explore a small part of this chain of lowlands. Beginning in Quebec, Canada, and stretching all the way to Alabama, the valley once provided easy passage for Native Americans to journey north and south, and later became a key railroad corridor for transporting the region's agricultural bounty to markets well beyond the Catskills.

A nearly level hike along the Wallkill Valley Rail Trail leads through farmland planted with corn and beans, orchards loaded with ripening apples, and pastures for cattle and horses. The Shawangunk Grasslands introduce new birders to a world of open land birding, featuring dozens of pairs of bobolinks, all manner of grassland sparrows, and nesting American kestrels. The John Burroughs Nature Sanctuary and Shaupeneak Ridge provide easier hikes with wetlands and waterfalls, just the thing for younger children discovering woodlands, marshes, and wildflowers.

We offer a selection of hikes that introduce you to this region's vast resources—enough to help you begin to explore on your own and find the hiking experiences that are right for you and your family. No book can cover every one of the dozens of hikes in this region, so consider this a sampling of the kinds of experiences you can enjoy during a visit to Ulster County.

28 SHAUPENEAK RIDGE COOPERATIVE RECREATION AREA

This oak, hickory, and hemlock forest hides treats within its depths: two little waterfalls and a delightful view all the way to the Hudson River.

County: Ulster
Start: Lower parking area on Old Post Road, just west of Esopus
Elevation gain: 685 feet
Distance: 3.2 miles out and back
Difficulty: Moderate
Hiking time: About 2 hours
Seasons: Spring and summer
Schedule: Open daily, dawn to dusk
Fees and permits: No fees or permits required
Trail contact: Scenic Hudson, One Civic Center Plaza, Ste. 200, Poughkeepsie 12601; (845) 473-4440; scenichudson.org/parks/shaupeneakridge

Canine compatibility: Dogs permitted on 6-foot leash; please carry out waste.
Trail surface: Dirt and rock
Land status: Scenic Hudson Land Trust
Nearest town: Esopus, New York
Other trail users: Trail runners
Maps: NatGeo TOPO! Map (USGS): Hyde Park, NY; trail map available online at scenichudson.org/sites/default/files/shaupeneak-2016_webmap.jpg
Special considerations: Hunting takes place here in spring and fall, so wear blaze orange—or consider hiking at another time.

FINDING THE TRAILHEAD

From the north or south, cross the Mid-Hudson Bridge (US 44) from east to west. Take US 9W north for 8.2 miles to Old Post Road; turn left. Continue 0.2 mile to the lower parking lot and the White Trailhead. Trailhead GPS: N41 49.624' / W73 58.213'

THE HIKE

Scenic Hudson owns and manages the 936.5-acre Shaupeneak Ridge Cooperative Recreation Area, where 3.5 miles of nicely marked and maintained trails provide adventures in several different kinds of habitats. This hike to two waterfalls and a wide view of the eastern Catskills takes you through second-growth forest and over rocky terrain to a merrily flowing creek, where a good rain creates a bubbling cascade at one juncture and a delicately trickling curtain falls at another.

Once you've seen the falls, your exploration continues. The White Trail climbs to the crest of Shaupeneak Ridge, a 25-mile stretch along the Marlboro Mountains from Newburgh to Kingston, with its high point at 892 feet. The view from the ridge differs from the more standard Hudson River fare, with farmland and dense woodland between you and the river itself. It's worth the effort, however, so if you're up for gaining another 600 feet in elevation, you'll find a nice reward at the top.

Locals know Shaupeneak for its wildlife as much as for its water features and views. Beavers, coyotes, and white-tailed deer are frequently spotted, as are individuals and flocks of wild turkeys—a particularly impressive sight in spring, when the males fan their tails

Take this moderate trail through rocky but pleasant woods.

and display their bright blue heads to attract mates among the far more prevalent females. A spring walk here can yield a wide variety of perching birds (known as passerines to experienced birders): blue-winged, black-and-white, hooded, magnolia, chestnut-sided, black-throated green, and black-throated blue warblers, as well as northern parula, common yellowthroat, scarlet tanager, and rose-breasted grosbeak.

Top: The ridgetop reveals an unusual view, featuring the Hudson River.
Bottom: This curtain falls appears on the purple-blazed side trail.

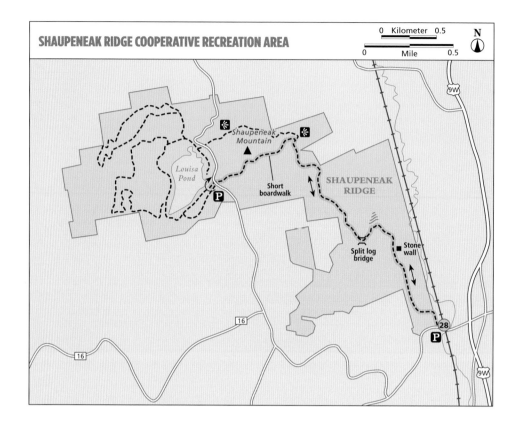

MILES AND DIRECTIONS

0.0 Start from the parking area and follow the White Trail. (There is only one trailhead here.)

0.5 Pass a stone wall.

0.7 The Purple Trail goes right. Take this trail to the waterfalls. In a few moments, you'll see the first falls, a curtain flowing over moss-covered rocks. When you're ready, return to the main trail by following the Purple Trail back the way you came. Continue up the White Trail.

0.8 Come to the second waterfall, just off the White Trail. It's a smaller but more dramatic cascade. When you're ready, continue uphill on the White Trail.

1.6 Reach the ridgetop and the overlook point at the end of the White Trail. Look east to see the Hudson River in the distance, as well as a splendid view of the surrounding highlands. Return the way you came, down the White Trail. (**Option:** You can add 2.4 miles by taking the Red Trail loop west to where it meets the Blue Trail, circling Louisa Pond on the Blue Trail and returning on the Red Trail.)

3.2 Arrive back at the trailhead.

29 JOHN BURROUGHS NATURE SANCTUARY

Hike in the footsteps of one of the state's most legendary naturalists, through a varied landscape of ridgelines, vernal pools, swamp, waterfalls, and ancient rock.

County: Ulster
Start: Small parking area off Burroughs Drive, which is off Floyd Ackert Road in West Park
Elevation gain: 238 feet
Distance: 2.0-mile loop with optional add-ons
Difficulty: Easy
Hiking time: About 1.5 hours
Seasons: Spring through fall
Schedule: Open daily, dawn to dusk
Fees and permits: No fees or permits required
Trail contact: John Burroughs Association, 261 Floyd Ackert Rd., PO Box 439, West Park 12493; (845) 384-6320; johnburroughsassociation .org

Canine compatibility: Dogs permitted on leash
Trail surface: Dirt, some stone steps
Land status: Owned and maintained by the John Burroughs Association
Nearest town: West Park, New York
Other trail users: People touring Burroughs' cottage (Slabsides)
Maps: John Burroughs Nature Sanctuary trail guide (johnburroughs association.org/images/documents/ TrailGuide.pdf)
Special considerations: You can see Slabsides from the outside anytime, but if you want to tour the cabin, check the John Burroughs Association website for scheduled tour dates.

FINDING THE TRAILHEAD

From I-87, take exit 18 to New Paltz. At the end of the ramp, follow NY 299 East, and turn left on US 9W. Drive 3.7 miles, and look for the "Path through History" signs at the intersection of Floyd Ackert Road and US 9W in West Park; turn left onto Floyd Ackert Road (at Global Palate restaurant). In 0.8 mile, turn left on Burroughs Drive. Continue for 0.3 mile to the trailhead sign. Park on the road and follow the signs to the trailhead. Trailhead GPS: N41 47.973' / W73 58.311'

THE HIKE

John Burroughs's name may not be familiar to you if you haven't spent much of your life reading nonfiction nature authors of the late nineteenth and early twentieth centuries. To those of us who relish narratives about the natural world, however, Burroughs rises to the level of legend. How wonderful that we have the opportunity to see where he lived and worked 120 to 150 years ago, much as it was when he owned this property.

Born in 1837 and raised on his family's farm in Delaware County, John Burroughs developed his love of nature while working outdoors in fields overlooking Slide Mountain and other Catskills peaks. His career as an essayist began in 1860 with publication in the *Atlantic Monthly*, supporting himself in professions related to finance while composing his writings about his own observations and perceptions of nature. His essays helped him form a strong bond with poet Walt Whitman, which led Burroughs to write Whitman's biography and literary criticism of his poems; this in turn led publisher Hurd

Naturalist John Burroughs made Slabsides his writing retreat.

& Houghton to contract with Burroughs to publish his first full book of essays about nature, *Wake-Robin*, in 1871.

Learning early on that writing about nature does not pay a living wage, Burroughs engaged in a more profitable career as a federal bank examiner in Washington, DC, and later in New York City. Burroughs used his earnings to purchase a 9-acre farm back in his home state in what is now Esopus; he called it Riverby because of its position on the west bank of the Hudson River. Here he lived with his wife, Ursula North, experimented with a number of crops before settling on table grapes as his focus, and spent his leisure time on his own writing. Eventually he bought additional land adjoining Riverby, where in 1895 he built Slabsides, the small cabin that remains here at the nature sanctuary that bears his name.

Slabsides became Burroughs's writing retreat, a place for him to compose his essays in peace while growing celery in his own front yard—the aptly named Celery Swamp you will see on your hike through this sanctuary. Far from a recluse, however, Burroughs entertained often at this little cabin and joined many fabulously wealthy friends on their explorations of the region and beyond. Theodore Roosevelt, Thomas Edison, Harvey Firestone, John Muir, and Henry Ford all called Burroughs a friend—in fact, Ford presented Burroughs with one of the first automobiles in the Hudson Valley for his personal use. Today Slabsides is a National Historic Landmark, and is listed in the National Register of Historic Places.

It might seem that a man who wrote and published his own musings about the natural world would avoid controversy, but Burroughs leapt into debate with both feet. He himself triggered what became known as the "nature fakers controversy," an ongoing denouncement of nature writers who wrote overblown, obviously imaginative accounts

Recent trail updates like these stone steps make this an easy hike.

of encounters with wildlife. Burroughs objected to works that anthropomorphized animals, giving them the capacity to display humanlike emotions or assuming that they have motivations like anger, jealousy, resentment, revenge, and love. He published an article in the *Atlantic Monthly* calling out famous authors including Ernest Thompson and William J. Long, accusing them of "yellow journalism of the woods" in portraying animals as if they were people on four legs. This controversy continued in the press for nearly six years, until Burroughs's friend Roosevelt—by then president of the United States—wrote an essay siding with Burroughs. The president titled his essay "Nature Fakers," and this label stuck with these writers for the long term. (With the modern use of animals as humanlike characters in movies, children's books, and advertising, this controversy has long since faded into distant memory.)

What makes Burroughs's works so compelling? The vast majority of them are written from his personal experience, whether they are about climbing Slide or Peekamoose Mountain or Millbrook Ridge, rafting the Delaware River, or trout fishing the Catskills' many rivers and lakes. His essays on speckled trout have become canon among the region's anglers. Officials in the Catskills celebrated his contribution to nature literature—and its contribution to tourism—by naming the ridge formed by Slide, Cornell, and Wittenberg Mountains the "Burroughs Range" and placing a plaque bearing one of his quotes about Slide on an outcrop on the mountain itself.

Visitors can see Slabsides from the outside anytime as you enter the nature preserve, but tours are offered only twice a year on Open House Days, the first Saturday in May and October (for more information, visit research.amnh.org/burroughs/programs.html). The tours are worth waiting for, as the cabin remains much as Burroughs left it. It's easy

to imagine the author at the writing desk within its bark-covered log walls, working with pen and paper and referencing the books that still fill the shelves.

On any other day, you can walk the trails through this 170-acre preserve and enjoy recent improvements made with the help of a grant from the New York State Office of Parks, Recreation and Historic Preservation. Volunteers constructed stone paths, stairways to high spots along the trails, and a boardwalk that crosses the deep muck in the Celery Swamp—much to the relief of frequent visitors. If you spot a trail worker during your visit, be sure to thank them for their efforts.

MILES AND DIRECTIONS

0.0 Start from the parking area and take the dirt/crushed stone trail in front of you. Pass a private drive and continue on the trail to your left.

0.2 The Ridge Trail begins. The building on your right is Slabsides, which is open only on specific tour dates. Celery Swamp begins on your right; the ridgeline's rock formations appear on the left.

0.3 Stone steps go up to your left; these lead to Julian's Rock. Take this side trail (option) or continue to the right, where a boardwalk crosses a spring. White trail markers begin here.

0.9 Stone steps lead down toward the red-blazed trail.

1.0 The orange-blazed trail (Ladder Trail) goes left here. The Chodikee Trail to Pond House goes right. If you wish to take the Ladder Trail here, it connects to the Chodikee Trail shortly so you can complete the loop.

1.1 Reach the intersection of the Ridge Trail with the Chodikee Trail. Continue on the Chodikee (red-blazed) trail.

Above: Columbine is one of dozens of native wildflowers that grow in this sanctuary.
Facing page: Follow the boardwalk across this pond for excellent views.

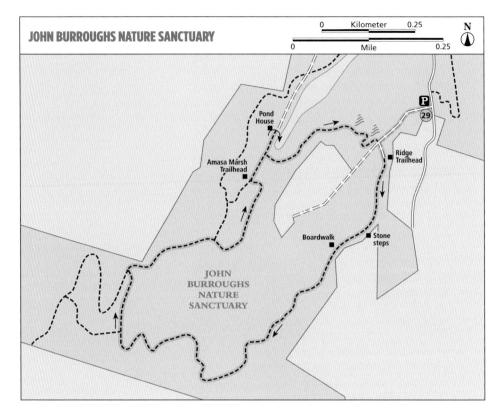

0   Kilometer   0.25

0   Mile   0.25

N

1.2 The trail forks here, and an unmarked trail goes left. The red-blazed trail continues right; go right. Soon a pond comes into view on the left.

1.4 The Amasa Marsh Trail (green markers) goes left here. The red-blazed trail continues straight; go straight.

1.5 At the pond, a trail with yellow markers goes right. Continue straight on the red-blazed trail to see the Pond House, then return here and take the yellow-blazed trail to complete the loop.

1.7 Cross two streams on big slabs of rock, then take stone steps to view a series of waterfalls.

1.8 At the top of the stairs, you have returned to the gravel road on which you came in. Turn left to return to the parking area.

2.0 Arrive back at the parking area.

30 BONTICOU CRAG

A challenging hike—with the option of some serious rock climbing—that leads to a spectacular view.

County: Ulster
Start: Spring Farm Trailhead and parking area, 50 Upper 27 Knolls Rd., High Falls
Elevation gain: 488 feet
Distance: 3.4-mile loop
Difficulty: Moderate to strenuous. (You have a choice of two routes.)
Hiking time: About 2 hours
Seasons: Spring through fall
Schedule: Open daily, sunrise to 1 hour after sunset
Fees and permits: Per-person fee to hike from the Mohonk Preserve trailheads
Trail contact: Mohonk Preserve, PO Box 715, New Paltz 12561; (845) 255-0919; mohonkpreserve.org
Canine compatibility: Dogs permitted on leash, but leave your dog at home if you plan to climb the scramble.
Trail surface: Dirt and rock
Land status: Nonprofit nature preserve
Nearest town: New Paltz, New York
Other trail users: Mountain bikers, rock climbers, trail runners
Maps: Mohonk Lake Region hiking map (mohonk.com/wp-content/uploads/2018/04/Mohonk-Hiking-Map-Guest-18.pdf)
Special considerations: This trail involves some tight squeezes and scrambling up rock faces; you have the option of skipping the most-strenuous sections and taking an easier route. Some sections of the trail may be closed during peregrine falcon nesting season.

FINDING THE TRAILHEAD

Take the New York State Thruway to exit 18 (New Paltz). Head west on NY 299 (through New Paltz); go over a steel bridge and turn right onto Springtown Road then take a left onto Mountain Rest Road. Pass the entrance to the Mohonk Mountain House and go under the one-lane bridge. Continue for 1 mile and turn right on Upper 27 Knolls Road. Within 0.25 mile you'll reach the kiosk for the Spring Farm Trailhead. This is the trailhead for Bonticou Crag and the Table Rocks Trail. Trailhead GPS: N41 79.373' / W74 12.869'

THE HIKE

The Shawangunk Mountains (or the Gunks) are a ridge of bedrock that runs from the northernmost tip of New Jersey to the Catskill Mountains. Bonticou Crag is part of the Gunks, which are known as one of the best climbing areas in the United States.

You don't have to do the hand-over-hand climb on the rock scramble when you reach it—there is a gentler ascent—but if you're up for a challenge, it's worth the effort.

Before you start the hike, make a pitstop to see the "Million Dollar View" from the area just above and to the left of the parking lot. Soak up the spectacular view of the Catskill Mountains, including Overlook and Hunter and the Escarpment Trail. Then head back along a dirt road to follow the red-blazed Bonticou Crag Trail. You'll cross an open meadow filled with milkweed in summer. The path becomes shadier, and the trail is a gradual uphill climb until you hit a short descent to the base of the scramble. If you're not up for this scramble, you can bail out on your left and take the trail around to get to the summit.

Conquer the scramble: focus on the red-blazed directions, narrow your concentration, and be patient. You can hike around, if you don't want to climb up.

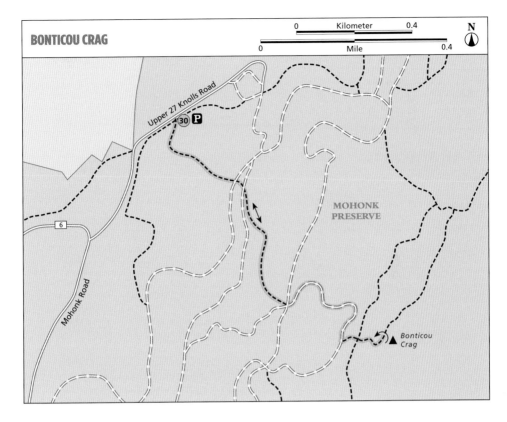

Before you start the scramble, take a few minutes to just be awed. The large rocks and boulders look as if they were thrown down by an angry god. The rocks are painted with red blazes so you can find your way to the top. Don't try this if the weather is bad; the angled rocks will be slippery. It will take all your concentration to move from one spot to another. If you know someone who has already done this hike, you might ask them to come along to help with hand and foot placement.

Once you hit the summit, you're rewarded with breathtaking north and west views of the Catskills—and possibly a few vultures.

At the top of the crag—360-degree views of Walkill Valley, the Shawangunks, and the Catskills.

BONTI WHO?

According to the Daniel Smiley Research Center at the Mohonk Preserve, the word "Bonticou" comes from the Dutch *Bonte kow*, meaning "the spotted cow." This was the name of a ship that brought Huguenot families to America. Originally the name referred to the farm and fields along the Wallkill River. "Crag" comes from the Celtic for a rugged cliff or rock face.

MILES AND DIRECTIONS

0.0   Leave the parking lot and follow red markers for the Bonticou Crag Trail. (This is also the trailhead for the Table Rocks Trail.)

0.37 Cross Cedar Drive and then Spring Farm Road (gravel). Stay on the Bonticou Crag Trail for a gradual uphill walk. You'll be walking around the edges of a meadow.

0.6   Cross Cedar Drive (again, as it's a loop). This is a very confusing intersection. Continue following the red markers. Take the wide left turn (not the hard left onto Cedar Drive) to continue on the Bonticou Crag Trail.

1.0   Go left on Bonticou Road. You'll go downhill a few hundred yards to the base of the scramble and a sign saying "Bonticou Rock Scramble" with a red marker. The scramble takes about 15 to 20 minutes to climb. The rocky trail is marked by red blazes. (**Option:** Take a left at the base of the scramble; follow the signs for Bonticou Footpath (yellow-blazed trail) and go around the rock scramble to get to the summit.) If you came up the scramble, turn back onto the yellow-blazed Bonticou Footpath. There are lots of roots and rocks as you head downhill.

1.89 Junction with northeast trail. Stay on the Bonticou Footpath. A typed sign in a tree trunk reads "Return to Spring Farm Trailhead." Begin to follow the light blue blazes.

2.38 You're back to the base of the scramble. Turn right and head back to the parking lot.

3.38 Arrive back at the trailhead.

31 MILLBROOK RIDGE

Enjoy New York State's largest member-supported nature preserve and amazing views of the Catskill Mountains from just outside the state park's borders.

County: Ulster
Start: East Trapps Trailhead at Mohonk Preserve
Elevation gain: 1,194 feet
Distance: 7.0-mile lollipop
Difficulty: Moderate
Hiking time: About 4 hours
Seasons: Year-round
Schedule: Trailheads open daily at 7 a.m. for members and 9 a.m. for day-use visitors. The visitor center is open 9 a.m. to 5 p.m. daily. Preserve lands and trailheads close at sunset.
Fees and permits: Fee to hike Mohonk Preserve's trails; separate fee for cyclists, climbers, and horseback riders. Children under 12 are admitted free. A basic annual membership is available for adults.
Trail contact: Mohonk Preserve, PO Box 715, New Paltz 12561; (845) 255-0919; mohonkpreserve.org

Canine compatibility: Dogs permitted on leash
Trail surface: Carriage roads, shale-surfaced, rocks, dirt
Land status: Nonprofit nature preserve
Nearest town: New Paltz, New York
Other trail users: Cyclists, horseback riders, and climbers on nearby trails
Maps: Mohonk Preserve Millbrook Ridge (mohonkpreserve.org/wp-content/uploads/2021/07/WT_SuggestedHike_MILLBROOK_MAP_6.14.21.pdf)
Special considerations: Since this preserve is only 90 minutes from New York City, it is extremely crowded on weekends. Get there early to find parking; better yet, go during the week.

FINDING THE TRAILHEAD

To reach the visitor center: From the New York State Thruway, take exit 18 for New Paltz. Go 7 miles west (through New Paltz) on NY 299 to the end. Turn right on US 44/NY 55 and then drive 0.5 mile to the visitor center, on the right. If that lot is full, continue a few hundred yards farther uphill to additional, overflow parking lots at the visitor center. The East Trapps Trailhead parking area is located at 3142 US 44 in Gardiner, about 1.3 miles past the visitor center. Trailhead GPS: N41 74.014' / W74 19.991'

THE HIKE

Back in 1869, identical twin brothers Albert and Alfred Smiley bought Lake Mohonk in Ulster County and built the Mohonk Mountain House resort. The brothers began with just 300 acres of land and would ultimately own 3,500 acres, a swath of land about 1 mile wide and 6 miles long running across the crest of the mountains. They created 40 miles of private roads and 25 miles of walks. They also owned Minnewaska Lake and 2,500 acres of land about 7 miles from Mohonk.

Nearly a century later, the Smiley family, friends, and supporters created the Mohonk Trust to protect the natural landscape and preserve more than 5,000 acres as forever wild. Today the resort, which resembles a Victorian castle, is known for its luxe accommodations and amazing setting high above the Hudson Valley, with a panoramic vista that includes forest, the Catskill Mountains, and Shawangunk Cliffs.

Top: Steep and rocky start for the first quarter mile.
Bottom: Watch your footing on the narrow ridge before you reach the summit.

The Mohonk Preserve is located on the Shawangunk Ridge, part of the Appalachian Mountains. There are 70 miles of carriage roads and 40 miles of trails for hiking, biking, running, cross-country skiing, snowshoeing, rock climbing, and horseback riding.

Whether you're staying at the hotel or not, there is a fee to park and to use the trails, with the money going to support landscape maintenance and educational programs.

MILLBROOK RIDGE

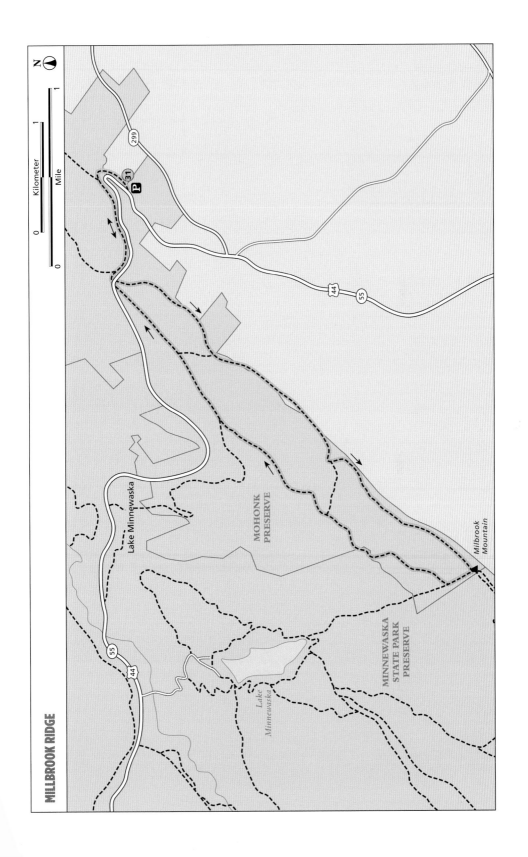

The challenging hike pays off with an incredible view of the Hudson Valley.

Start your hiking day with a quick stop at the visitor center to pay for a pass and get the lay of the land by looking at a large three-dimensional trail map. You can also get free trail maps and use the facilities. Then drive about 1 mile to the East Trapps Trailhead parking area.

The first 0.25 mile of your journey is going to be rocky and steep. As you chug up the hill, you're treated to glimpses of the Catskills and the Hudson Valley. Soon you'll be walking along the spine of the ridge, which can get narrow at times. Stop along the way to pick handfuls of blueberries in season. You'll see hemlock and dwarf pitch pine.

Once at the top, with a wide-open view, you'll feel as if you're seated just under the clouds. There are falcons, eagles, and vultures. Hawks float by on the air currents. Rest and enjoy the view. Your way back will be along a wide, nicely forested carriage road.

If it's warm and you need to refresh, drive over to Split Rock swimming hole (about 1 mile away on Clove Road from NY 55/US 44). There's a parking area across the street from the swimming hole. *Caution:* This is not an "official" swimming area, and there's no lifeguard.

Note: If you're doing further research on this hike, don't confuse it with the Mill Brook Ridge Trail that is accessed by the Alder Lake Trailhead in Livingston Manor, about 70 miles from Mohonk Preserve's Millbrook Ridge Trail.

MILES AND DIRECTIONS

0.0 Park at the East Trapps Trailhead and follow signs to cross at the bridge over US 44/NY55 to the East Trapps Connector Trail (yellow markers). The trail leads to a network of more than 100 miles of carriage roads and trails and to the West Trapps climbing cliffs. (*Note:* The East Trapps Connector Trail is closed during winter.)

0.7 Turn left at the junction of Undercliff/Overcliff Roads and the Millbrook Ridge Trail (light blue blazes).

1.2 Bayards Path (red blazes) is on the right. (*Option:* If you need a bailout, you can take this trail down to Trapps Road, a parallel carriage road, and head back to the parking lot.) Stay on the light blue-blazed trail.

2.3 The Millbrook Cross Trail (red blazes) is on the right. (*Option:* Follow it if you want to get back to the carriage road.) Stay on the blue-blazed trail.

2.7 Reach a field of rocks and boulders; stay alert for blue blazes on rocks and trees.

2.8 Head up on a rock scramble for about 5 minutes.

3.6 Junction of blue- and red-blazed trails. Go a few yards past the junction sign to reach the summit and a magnificent 360-degree view. Return to the main trail and turn right on the red-blazed trail. (*Options:* At the red-blazed trail, you can hike to Lake Minnewaska (about 2.0 miles one way). Or, instead of turning at all, you can continue through on the Millbrook Ridge Trail to Gertrude's Nose).

3.9 Turn right on the Coxing Trail and follow the blue blazes.

5.6 Bear right on Trapps Road, a flat carriage road.

6.7 You're back to the bridge; head back to the parking lot.

7.0 Arrive back at the trailhead.

32 GERTRUDE'S NOSE/ MINNEWASKA TRAIL

Hike these amazing Shawangunk rock formations to arrive at what feels like standing on the prow of a ship high above the world.

County: Ulster
Start: Minnewaska State Park Preserve, Upper Awosting lot, 5281 US 44/NY55, Kerhonkson
Elevation gain: 1,135 feet
Distance: 7.5-mile lollipop
Difficulty: Moderate to strenuous
Hiking time: About 5 hours
Seasons: Year-round
Schedule: Open daily at 9 a.m.
Fees and permits: Fee per vehicle; Empire Pass accepted
Trail contact: Minnewaska State Park Preserve, 5281 US 44/NY55; Kerhonkson 12446; (845) 255-0752

Canine compatibility: Dogs permitted on leash
Trail surface: Graded carriage roads, rocks, roots, boulders
Land status: New York State Park
Nearest town: New Paltz, New York
Other trail users: Rock climbers; snowshoers (in season)
Maps: Minnewaska State Park Preserve (parks.ny.gov/documents/parks/MinnewaskaMinnewaska StateParkTrailMap.pdf)
Special considerations: Proximity to New York City makes this a popular weekend destination.

FINDING THE TRAILHEAD

From New Paltz, head west on NY 299. Follow NY 299 until it dead-ends into US 44/NY55 and turn right. Follow US 44/NY 55 past the hairpin turn under the Shawangunk Cliffs and past the Trapps Trailhead parking area on your right. Continue another 3 miles past the Trapps parking area to find the well-marked entrance to Minnewaska State Park Preserve on your left. Stop at the guard shack, pay the fee, then turn left and continue uphill until you reach the upper parking lot. Trailhead GPS: N41 73.051' / W74 23.419'

THE HIKE

Minnewaska State Park Preserve is located on the Shawangunk Mountains ridge, which rises more than 2,000 feet above sea level. The park's 24,000 acres includes waterfalls, streams, three lakes, hardwood forest, sheer cliffs and ledges, 35 miles of carriage roads, and 50 miles of footpaths.

Before heading out to hike, spend a few minutes at the beautiful, modern Lake Minnewaska Visitor Center, where you can learn about conservation efforts, rock formations, and park history, as well as fill your water bottle, use the restroom, and charge your phone. The LEED-certified building is a testament to sustainable design using passive solar and natural ventilation concepts. The building has bird-friendly glass to reduce bird strikes and rain gardens to manage stormwater runoff. It was built by New York State in partnership with the Open Space Institute.

The hike along Gertrude's Nose is one of the preserve's most spectacular. The hike is named for Gertrude Bruyn, a Dutch settler who, in the 1680s, lived on the west bank of the Shawangunk Kill, across the water from the eponymous cliff escarpment. Local lore has it that the shadows of the massive rocks that stand on the brow of the mountain resemble Bruyn's nose.

In hot weather, hikers appreciate the cool air wafting up from the crevasses. In winter, if covered in snow, they pose a danger.

You get views of Lake Minnewaska and the cliffs across the way as soon as you start hiking the wide gravel carriage road. The trail turns more rugged as you hike, and you'll soon be walking over or around glacial erratics, such as Patterson's Pellet. Glacial erratics are rocks that were transported by glaciers and left behind when the glaciers melted. On this trail, that was about 12,000 years ago. The great views are just beginning.

From here you can see over the Palmaghatt Ravine—a wilderness valley separating the Millbrook Mountain–Gertrude's Nose ridge from the main ridge to the west. It's well known as one of the most scenic views in the Shawangunks.

Eventually you'll arrive at an even rockier part of the path. Channel your inner mountain goat and pick your way along carefully.

There are enticing outcroppings and more great views as you hike, but watch your footing over the small and large crevices, tight vertical fissures, between the large rocks. In October 2021, a hiker's dog became trapped in a crevice, where she remained for five days—licking moisture off the rock walls to keep herself alive—before being rescued by the volunteer New Jersey Initial Response Team.

Once you reach the tip of the nose, you're rewarded with a majestic 270-degree view, including an unobstructed view of the Hudson Valley. Be prepared for a few rocky climbs after you continue around to complete the loop.

MILES AND DIRECTIONS

0.0 Start from the parking area and bear left onto a dirt road. Turn right on the red-blazed Minnewaska Carriage Road. (This circles the lake.) Soon you'll reach a junction with the Upper Awosting Carriage Road. Stay on the Minnewaska Carriage Road.

0.44 Junction with the Castle Point Trail, on the right. Stay on the red-blazed trail.

0.79 Bear right at a junction and follow the yellow blazes.

1.0 Bear left at the fork with the Hamilton Point Carriage Road. Follow the yellow blazes.

1.5 Reach Patterson's Pellet.

The white cliff edges of Gertrude's Nose in the Shawangunks.

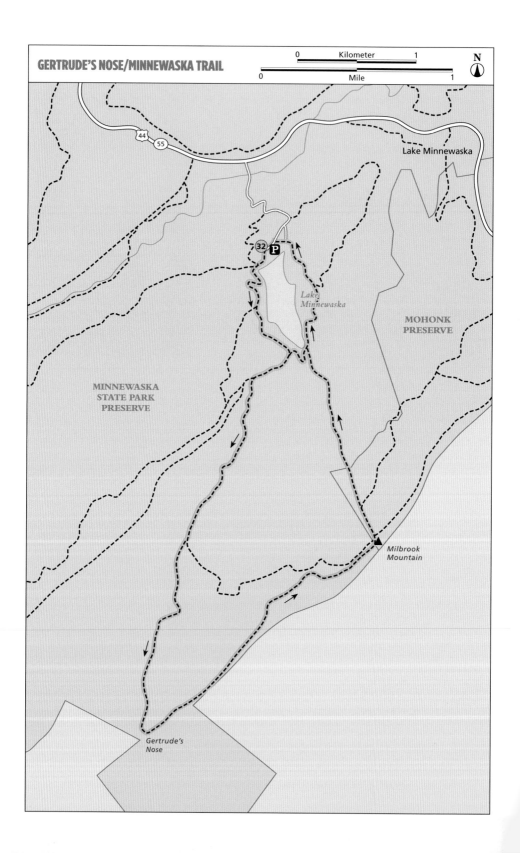

0   Kilometer   1

0   Mile   1

N

44
55

Lake Minnewaska

32 P

Lake
Minnewaska

MOHONK
PRESERVE

MINNEWASKA
STATE PARK
PRESERVE

Milbrook
Mountain

Gertrude's
Nose

Beneath the jagged white cliffs, the mile-long Lake Minnewaska has several designated swimming areas.

2.0 Bear right on the red-blazed trail, the Gertrude's Nose Footpath. You're walking along a ridgeline with a cliff on your right. Be careful as you enjoy great views.

2.4 There are two red blazes on a tree. The blazes show you the direction the trail turns. Bear right.

2.6 The trail turns left. Yes, those are power lines you're seeing and hiking under. Continue following the red blazes.

3.3 Reach the tip of the "nose." Follow the red blazes to complete the loop.

5.0 You can stay on the rocky trail or take the yellow-blazed gravel trail on the left (parallel to the red-blazed trail) for a short respite before a steep rocky climb to the end.

5.1 Come to a fork in the road/dead end. You're at the Millbrook Mountain Path. Go a little farther and the trail veers left. Follow the red blazes.

5.2 "Lake Minnewaska" sign. Turn left as the path descends; follow the red blazes.

5.3 Several trails converge. Follow the sign for Lake Minnewaska, looking for the red blazes. Continue descending; watch your footing—the trail may be wet.

5.6 Cross a stream and begin your ascent.

5.8 Climb a steep rocky path, following red blazes, for 15 minutes.

6.4 Gravel carriage trail and the end of Minnewaska Lake. Turn right and follow the red-blazed trail, with the lake on your left. Only members can swim in this part of the lake. Continue uphill, picking out the red blazes. As you go around the curve, go up and around a red blaze; don't take the hard right.

6.7 On your left is an open meadow with picnic tables, shady trees, and great views. Cross the field to head back to the visitor center. Take the wide carriage trail, following the red blazes. From here it's about a 10-minute walk to the visitor center and parking area.

7.5 Arrive back at the parking area.

An easy hike anyone at any age or stage can enjoy, with beautiful scenery and the chance to watch—or participate in—some of the best rock climbing in the United States.

County: Ulster
Start: East Trapps Trailhead at Mohonk Preserve
Elevation gain: 249 feet
Distance: 5.1-mile loop
Difficulty: Easy
Hiking time: 2.5 to 3 hours
Seasons: Year-round.
Schedule: Trailheads open daily at 7 a.m. for members and 9 a.m. for day-use visitors. The visitor center is open 9 a.m. to 5 p.m. daily. Preserve lands and trailheads close at sunset.
Fees and permits: Fees to hike Mohonk Preserve's trails; separate fee for cyclists, climbers, and horseback riders. Children under 12 are admitted free. There is also a basic annual membership for adults.
Trail contact: Mohonk Preserve, PO Box 715, New Paltz 12561; (845) 255-0919; mohonkpreserve.org

Canine compatibility: Dogs permitted on leash
Trail surface: Carriage roads, shale-surfaced, rocks, dirt
Land status: Nonprofit nature preserve
Nearest town: New Paltz, New York
Other trail users: Cyclists, trail runners; snowshoers, cross-country skiers (in season)
Maps: mohonkpreserve.org/file _download/inline/3bd277ce-f6b1 -4095-bfb7-b4984e3772f8 or AllTrails Undercliff Overcliff Loop map (alltrails.com/explore/ recording/tue-25-aug-2020-18-57-f5deaee)
Special considerations: Since this preserve is only 90 minutes from New York City, it is extremely crowded on weekends. Get there early to find parking; better yet, go during the week.

FINDING THE TRAILHEAD

To reach the visitor center: From the New York State Thruway, take exit 18 for New Paltz. Go 7 miles west (through New Paltz) on NY 299 to the end. Turn right on US 44/NY 55 and then drive 0.5 mile to the visitor center, on the right. If that lot is full, continue a few hundred yards farther uphill to additional, overflow parking lots at the visitor center. The East Trapps Trailhead parking area is located at 3142 US 44, Gardiner, about 1.3 miles past the visitor center. Trailhead GPS: N41 73.715' / W74 19.751'

THE HIKE

Mohonk Mountain Preserve's mission is to protect the Shawangunk Mountains region. Known as "the Gunks," it's one of the oldest rock-climbing areas in the United States—and one of the best. One route, known as High Exposure, or "High E," was created by pioneer climbers Hans Kraus and Fritz Wiessner in 1941 and is a must-do among serious climbers.

The Gunks are mostly quartz, crystallized out of the groundwater in sediments deposited 430 million years ago. The rocks have long, vertical cracks called joints. There are tall blocks, some 120 feet high, with deep fissures and crevices between them. You can sometimes find fossils of armored fish and sea scorpions.

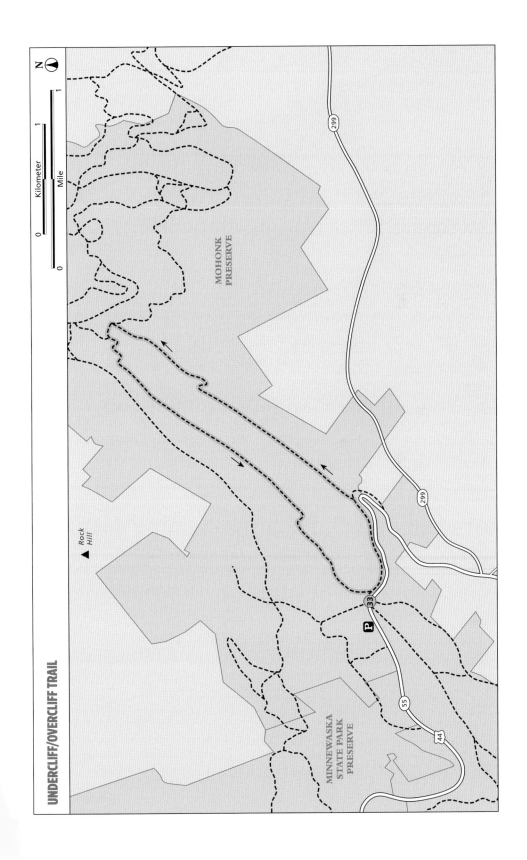

UNDERCLIFF/OVERCLIFF TRAIL

MOHONK PRESERVE

MINNEWASKA STATE PARK PRESERVE

Rock Hill

N

Kilometer

Mile

A climber warms up on the "gunks" on the Undercliff trail.

The entry to the Undercliff/Overcliff Trail, a relatively flat 5.0-mile loop.

The stark white Gunks offer more than 800 technical routes for every level of climber. The rocks, situated like a giant's game of Jenga, are spotted with chalk handhold marks. With its close proximity to New York City, only about 90 miles, the area is wildly popular. On any given weekend, there are hundreds of climbers belaying and bouldering.

Those not interested in climbing, however, can hike the 65 miles of trails in the preserve. The Undercliff/Overcliff path is part of a network of century-old carriage roads. It offers views of the climbers as you traverse a wide carriage road under the cliff. You'll catch glimpses of farms and the Wallkill River valley. Then you'll loop around to hike higher along the cliff (not quite "over" it). As you hike, you can catch glimpses of the Rondout Valley and Catskills peaks, particularly in leaf-off seasons. But it's hard to beat the beauty all around during September and October, when the fall colors rule.

MILES AND DIRECTIONS

0.0   Start from the eastern end of the parking area and follow the West Trapps Connector Trail, which leads east, parallel to US 44/NY 55.

0.3   Come to Trapps Bridge and a stairway leading up to the Undercliff and Overcliff Roads. The route basically takes you on a carriage road under the cliff and then returns (sort of) over the top of the cliff—or vice versa. Choose whichever way you'd like to travel. We went on Undercliff first (counterclockwise). Pass under a giant rock that nearly arches across the road.

2.5   Junction at Rhododendron Bridge and Laurel Ledge. Don't cross the bridge; instead turn left and follow the sign to Overcliff Road, bearing left. The road rises more steeply here. Stay on this road until you've completed the loop. Return to the parking lot.

5.1   Arrive back at the parking lot.

34 MINNEWASKA STATE PARK PRESERVE: MINNEWASKA LAKE CARRIAGE ROAD

Circle one of the prettiest sky lakes in the Hudson Valley region and discover Shawangunk geology.

County: Ulster
Start: Upper parking area at Lake Minnewaska, Minnewaska State Park Preserve
Elevation gain: 128 feet
Distance: 2.0-mile loop
Difficulty: Moderate
Hiking time: About 1.5 hours
Seasons: Spring through fall
Schedule: Open daily 9 a.m.; closing time varies with season. **Note:** This trail is closed to hiking in winter, when groomed for cross-country skiing. If snow conditions are not sufficient for skiing, the trail remains open for hiking.
Fees and permits: Entrance fee per vehicle
Trail contact: Minnewaska State Park Preserve, 5281 US 44/NY55, Kerhonkson 12446; (845) 255-0752; parks.ny.gov/parks/127/details.aspx

Canine compatibility: Dogs permitted on leash
Trail surface: Crushed stone
Land status: New York State Park Preserve
Nearest town: Kerhonkson, New York
Other trail users: Cyclists, equestrians; cross-country skiers (in season)
Maps: NatGeo TOPO! Map (USGS): Napanoch, NY; NatGeo Trails Illustrated Map #750: Shawangunk Mountains; New York–New Jersey Trail Conference Trail Map 104: Shawangunk Trails
Special considerations: While it's highly unlikely that you will encounter them, timber rattlesnakes and copperheads make their home in the park.

FINDING THE TRAILHEAD

From the south, take I-87 North to New Paltz (exit 18) and take NY 299 West (New Paltz–Minnewaska Road) about 7 miles to the end. Turn right on US 44/ NY 55 West and continue about 4.5 miles to the park preserve entrance. Once in the park, follow the signs for Lake Minnewaska and the upper parking area.

From the north, take I-87 to exit 18 and follow the directions above. Trailhead GPS: N41 43.732' / W74 14.227'

THE HIKE

Thank the perseverance of the State of New York for the existence of the gorgeous Minnewaska State Park Preserve, a portion of the estate owned by twin brothers Albert and Alfred Smiley. The Smileys owned this land as well as the neighboring Mohonk property, building resort hotels on each of the sites in the late 1800s—the still-popular Mohonk Mountain House and the 225-room Minnewaska Mountain House, or "Cliff House," as guests often called it. Alfred Smiley eventually managed Cliff House separately from his brother and built a second, larger hotel, Wildmere, on the Minnewaska property as well. Property manager Kenneth Phillips bought Cliff House from the Smileys in 1955, but

The Shawangunk Ridge dominates the skyline on the way to Minnewaska State Park Preserve.

Here's one of many viewpoints
on this lovely carriage road.

Minnewaska Lake provides plenty of beautiful views.

Shelters and benches alert hikers to some of the best viewpoints.

by 1972 the aging hotel had become overwhelmingly expensive to maintain. It stood abandoned until it burned to the ground in 1978; Wildmere burned as well in 1986.

Meanwhile, as the hotels stood empty and aging, New York State had been up to its proverbial elbows in proposals from developers, as well as counterproposals from environmentalists to keep the unique scenic area from becoming another housing tract or condominium complex. The state settled the matter in 1987 by buying the property and dedicating it as a state park. In 1993 New York changed the designation to State Park Preserve under Article 20 of the Parks, Recreation and Historic Preservation law. Three years later, the Open Space Institute acquired the area now known as Sam's Point Preserve and several thousand acres adjoining Minnewaska on its western boundary. Over the next two decades, all those lands became part of Minnewaska State Park Preserve.

In 2006, a plan to build 350 luxury homes on another 2,500 adjoining acres at the base of Shawangunk Ridge met fierce opposition from residents of nearby Gardiner, who formed a community activist group called Save the Ridge to battle the plan. Years of resistance finally led the developer to withdraw, making way for the sale of the parcel to the Trust for Public Land for a whopping $17 million. The Trust immediately made a gift of the land to New York State, further expanding the preserve.

The carriage road you will follow on this hike provides an introduction to the more than 35 miles of such paths in this park. You may enjoy another short hike from the parking area just past the entrance to this unit of the park: Awosting Falls, a meander of just under 1.0 mile along a creek to a dramatic waterfall. Carriage roads provide access to several delightful natural phenomena throughout the park, including Rainbow Falls, a 5.0-mile out-and-back hike from the same parking area as Awosting, with the payoff of a double waterfall (but only in spring or during very rainy summers).

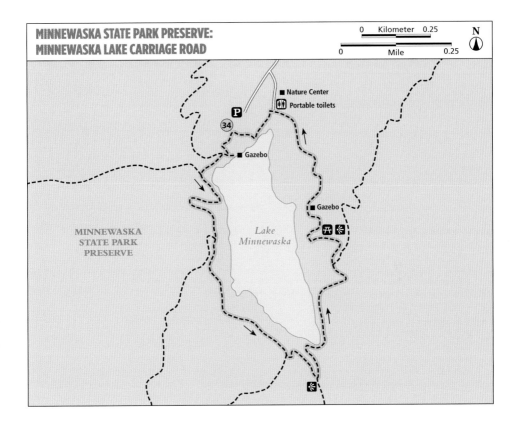

MILES AND DIRECTIONS

0.0 Start from the parking area and take the crushed-stone path to the lake. You'll see an interpretive sign for the Lake Minnewaska Carriage Road. Follow the red diamond-shaped markers. Turn right.

0.3 An unmarked path goes right. Bear left around the bend.

0.4 Castle Point Carriage Road goes right. Continue straight on the red-diamond trail.

0.8 The Millbrook Mountain Trail continues straight here. Go left on the red-diamond trail.

0.9 Reach the first great viewpoint of the lake.

1.0 At the end of the lake, you have a clear view of the entire area. The Millbrook Mountain footpath (red squares) starts here. Continue on the red-diamond path around the lake.

1.3 An unmarked trail goes right here. Continue straight on the red-diamond trail.

1.4 This is the top of the rock wall you saw from the parking area. There's a lilac grove here, a picnic area, and a spectacular view of the lake from the highest point on the trail and the site of the former Cliff House hotel.

1.5 A summer house (gazebo) offers more great views.

1.8 Come to some portable toilets. Just past these you'll find the nature center.

2.0 Arrive back at the parking area.

35 MINNEWASKA STATE PARK PRESERVE: RAINBOW FALLS

Enjoy a glistening curtain falls in spring in the midst of one of Ulster County's most dramatic landscapes.

County: Ulster
Start: Trailhead across from the Lake Awosting parking area, inside the main entrance to Minnewaska State Park Preserve
Elevation gain: 850 feet
Distance: 5.4 miles out and back
Difficulty: Strenuous
Hiking time: About 4 hours
Seasons: Spring and other times of high water
Schedule: Open daily at 9 a.m.; closing times posted at park entrances
Fees and permits: Entrance fee per vehicle
Trail contact: Minnewaska State Park Preserve, 5281 US 44/NY 55, Kerhonkson 12446; (845) 255-0752; parks.ny.gov/parks/minnewaska/details.aspx
Canine compatibility: Dogs permitted on leash no longer than 6 feet

Trail surface: Crushed-stone carriage road, dirt and woodland detritus
Land status: New York State Park Preserve
Nearest town: Kerhonkson, New York
Other trail users: Birders, runners, cyclists on the carriage road sections
Maps: Minnewaska State Park trails (parks.ny.gov/documents/parks/MinnewaskaMinnewaskaStateParkTrailMap.pdf)
Special considerations: Parking in the park is limited to 500 cars (though an expansion is planned), and it may fill up completely on summer weekends. Consider arriving early on summer and fall weekends or exploring this park on a weekday or in the off-season. No swimming is allowed at the falls. Swimming is permitted only at the Lake Minnewaska and Lake Awosting beaches, and then only when a lifeguard is on duty.

FINDING THE TRAILHEAD

From I-87, take exit 18 (New Paltz/NY 299). Drive west on NY 299 for 7.0 miles to the junction with US 44/NY 55. Turn right (west) onto US 44/NY 55 and continue for 4.5 miles to the park's main entrance. Turn left into Minnewaska State Park Preserve and continue to the Lake Awosting parking area. Trailhead GPS: N41 44.090' / W74 14.628'

THE HIKE

Actually two falls—the major flow is on the left, while a smaller falls flows on the right about 30 yards from the first—Rainbow Falls passes muster as one of the most magnificent waterfalls in Minnewaska State Park. It takes some effort to get to this most excellent sight, so many visitors don't make the trip, which means you may have the trail and the falls to yourself, particularly on a weekday at the height of spring.

The falls come at the end of a fairly strenuous hike that begins with a wide carriageway and eventually narrows along the edge of some steep rock faces. You'll climb about 275 feet in elevation as you navigate this trail. When you're going up, don't forget to look behind you to catch some panoramic views of the Catskill Mountains. We chose

MINNEWASKA STATE PARK PRESERVE: RAINBOW FALLS

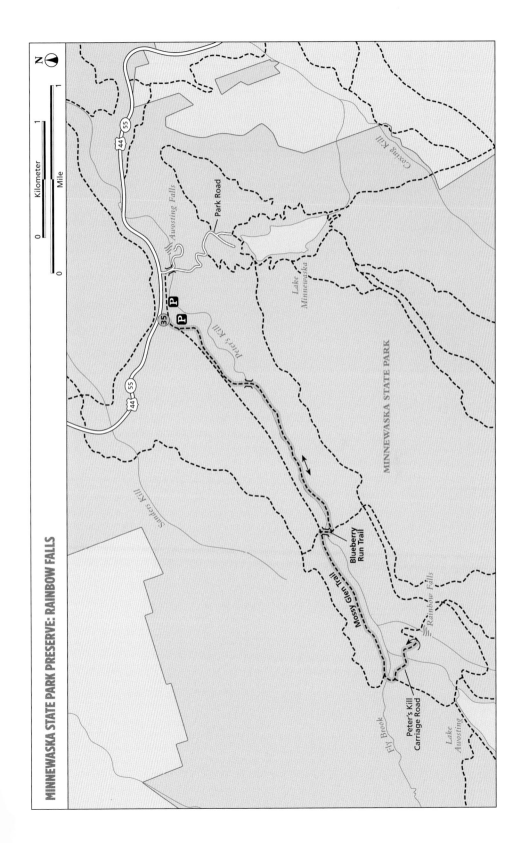

N

0   Kilometer   1

0   Mile   1

Awosting Falls

Park Road

44 55

35

P

P

Peter's Kill

Sanders Kill

Lake Minnewaska

Coxing Kill

MINNEWASKA STATE PARK

Mossy Glen Trail

Blueberry Run Trail

Fly Brook

Peter's Kill Carriage Road

Rainbow Falls

Lake Awosting

Carriage roads make hiking easier in Minnewaska State Park Preserve.

the out-and-back route rather than the longer loop trail back to the parking area, as the loop adds 3.0 miles to your hike. Minnewaska presents one terrific view after another, however, so if you want to make the most of your park experience, the longer trail may suit you. See the park's maps for details.

Before you take off down the carriage road to hike nearly 3.0 miles one way to see this waterfall, make sure there's more than a wet spot for you to see. Rainbow Falls flows lushly during the winter snowmelt and spring runoff seasons, but it can disappear altogether during the summer, and it may not reappear until the following year.

MILES AND DIRECTIONS

- **0.0** Start from the lower (Lake Awosting) parking area and take the Awosting Carriage Road to the southwest. Pass the Mossy Glen Trail intersection and continue on the carriage road.

- **0.7** Cross Peter's Kill and continue on the carriage road.

- **1.6** Come to an intersection with the Blueberry Run Trail. Turn right and cross a footbridge over Peter's Kill. In a few hundred feet, turn left onto the Mossy Glen Trail (yellow blazes).

- **2.4** Turn left onto Peter's Kill Carriage Road (black diamond markers). Continue to Rainbow Falls. As you approach the falls, scramble down some steep rock faces that may be slippery with spray.

- **2.7** Reach Rainbow Falls. When you're ready, return to the parking area the way you came.

- **5.4** Arrive back at the lower parking area.

36 MINNEWASKA STATE PARK PRESERVE: STONY KILL FALLS

A newly constructed trail provides unprecedented access to a waterfall previously known only to locals and falls baggers.

County: Ulster
Start: New parking area up the carriage road that begins on Shaft 2A Road, off Rock Haven Road in Minnewaska State Park Preserve
Elevation gain: 280 feet
Distance: 1.0 mile out and back
Difficulty: Moderate
Hiking time: About 1 hour
Seasons: Spring through fall
Schedule: Parking area open daily, 9 a.m. to 5 p.m.
Fees and permits: Entrance fee per vehicle to the park. (There may be no fee to enter the Stony Kill section.)
Trail contact: Minnewaska State Park Preserve, 5281 US 44/NY 55, Kerhonkson 12446; (845) 255-0752; parks.ny.gov/parks/minnewaska/details.aspx

Canine compatibility: Dogs permitted on leash no longer than 6 feet
Trail surface: Crushed-stone carriage road, stone steps, stone-paved sections
Land status: New York State Park Preserve
Nearest town: Kerhonkson, New York
Other trail users: Anglers, rock climbers
Maps: Minnewaska State Park trails (parks.ny.gov/documents/parks/MinnewaskaMinnewaskaStatePark TrailMap.pdf)
Special considerations: Timber rattlesnakes are found in this area, though they want nothing to do with humans. Watch your step, and wear boots with ankle protection.

FINDING THE TRAILHEAD

From I-87, take exit 18 (New Paltz/NY 299). Drive west on NY 299 for 7.0 miles to the junction with US 44/NY 55. Turn right (west) onto US 44/NY 55 and continue for 10 miles to Minnewaska Trail–Rock Haven Road. Turn left onto this road and then left again immediately onto Rock Haven Road. In about 2 miles, park at the end of Shaft 2A Road on either side of the gate, along the shoulder of the road. Do not block the gate. Trailhead GPS: N41 44.039' / W74 17.739'

THE HIKE

Since we first hiked to Stony Kill Falls for our *Hiking Waterfalls in New York*, this trail in the southwest corner of Minnewaska State Park Preserve has undergone a dramatic and much-appreciated change.

Stony Kill, one of four major streams in Minnewaska, incises a deep crevice in the Martinsburg Shale throughout this area, creating a stunning gorge riddled with massive shale slabs and impressive boulders. Here you have the opportunity to see layers of rock many millions of years old, revealed by the flowing water and glacial movement during the most-recent ice age.

What used to be a rock-scrambling challenge to reach, however, has now become a pleasant and far safer stroll along restored carriage roads, through a hemlock forest, and up finely hewn stone steps to a sturdy stone 12 × 12-foot viewing platform. Today's hikers can enjoy a stunning view of Stony Kill Falls, and then ascend an extra set of steps to

It's easy to see how Stony Kill got its name.

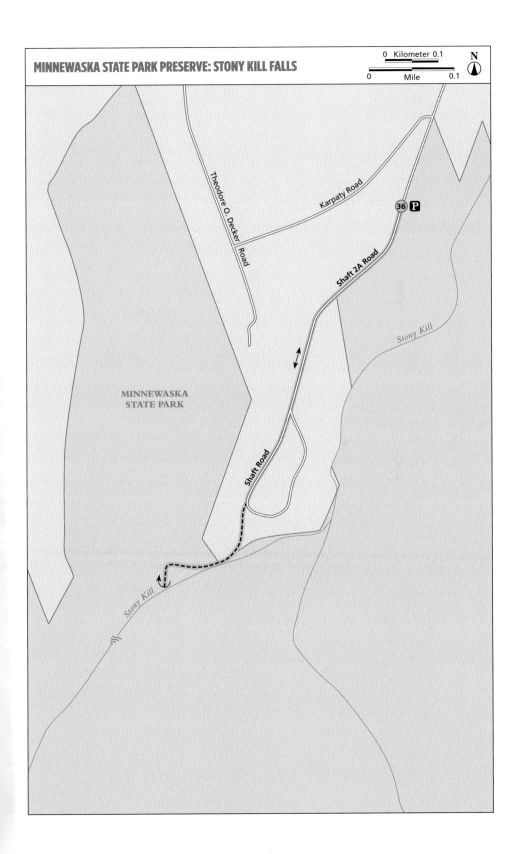

MINNEWASKA STATE PARK PRESERVE: STONY KILL FALLS

0   Kilometer   0.1

0   Mile   0.1

N

Theodore O. Decker Road

Karpaty Road

36 P

Shaft 2A Road

Stony Kill

MINNEWASKA
STATE PARK

Shaft Road

Stony Kill

stand parallel with the top of the falls, 87 feet above its plunge pool. In total, hikers will ascend 230 steps from the trail's lowest point to the top of the falls.

An extraordinary effort by a group known as the Jolly Rovers Trail Crew resulted in this gorgeous trail, which also includes two footbridges built by Tahawus Trails LLC—one 31 feet long; the other, 19 feet long. All of the stone used in the construction came from the immediate area's famous Shawangunk Conglomerate.

When the carriage roads found here were built for the enjoyment of wealthy neighbors and their guests, active shale mining provided the crushed stone that covered those roads, making use of the park's own resources for its maintenance. The quarry you see on this hike, however, did not provide that material to the park—it was privately owned by the Napanoch Sand and Gravel Company until 2001, when the State of New York joined forces with the Open Space Institute and the New York–New Jersey Trail Conference to acquire the land and preserve it permanently as part of Minnewaska State Park Preserve.

You also will see an aqueduct shaft as you drive up the carriage road at the beginning of the trail. This provides the City of New York with access to maintain the Catskill Aqueduct. Built between 1909 and 1915, the Catskill Aqueduct brought clear mountain water to residents of New York City, aided decades later by the Delaware Aqueduct. Together, these two subterranean waterways provide more than 350 million gallons of water to the city every day—a massive amount of water that represents less than 40 percent of the city's required daily supply. Four reservoirs in the region—Ashokan, Rondout, Pepacton, and Cannonsville—all retain the water that gets transported through these two aqueducts to the New York metropolitan area.

MILES AND DIRECTIONS

0.0 Start from the parking area and walk up the carriage road. Just before you reach the stream, the trail splits to the left. Follow the path to the right (watch for red markers on posts). Enter a hemlock woods and continue until you reach two bridges in succession over the stream. Cross the bridges and begin to ascend the first set of stone steps.

0.3 Reach the viewing platform, from which you have a clear view of Stony Kill Falls. You can enjoy the falls here and return the way you came or continue up the next set of steps to the top of the falls, 87 feet above you. Follow a series of switchbacks, stone-paved trail sections, and more steps. One short section provides iron railings and rungs to help you reach the top.

0.5 You have summited the falls. Here you can see the upper cascade up close, an additional 30 feet of rushing water before it tumbles over the edge and drops 87 feet. The trail continues from here into the woods on its way to the Stony Kill Carriage Road, but if you've achieved what you came for, return the way you came.

1.0 Arrive back at the parking area.

37 SHAWANGUNK GRASSLANDS NATIONAL WILDLIFE REFUGE

This grassland plays a critical role in protecting native plants and nesting bobolinks and kestrels—and you won't see another like it in New York State.

County: Ulster
Start: Parking area off Hoagerburgh Road in Wallkill
Elevation gain: 112 feet
Distance: 2.2-mile lollipop
Difficulty: Easy
Hiking time: About 1.5 hours
Seasons: Year-round
Schedule: Open daily, dawn to dusk
Fees and permits: No fees or permits required
Trail contact: Lenape National Wildlife Refuge Complex; (973) 702-7266; fws.gov/refuge/shawangunk_grasslands/
Canine compatibility: Dogs permitted on leash
Trail surface: Mowed grass

Land status: US Fish & Wildlife Service
Nearest town: Wallkill, New York
Other trail users: Birders, photographers, joggers, fitness walkers; cross-country skiers (in season)
Maps: Shawangunk Grasslands NWR (fws.gov/uploadedFiles/SG%20 habitat%20map.pdf)
Special considerations: This refuge is maintained as critical bird habitat year-round. Please stay on the trails to avoid stressing nesting bird species, including American kestrels in the nest box near the intersection of the red- and blue-blazed trails. Five blinds are provided for observing birds and other wildlife.

FINDING THE TRAILHEAD

From I-84, take exit 28 (formerly exit 5) for NY 208. Take NY 208 North to Walden. At the stoplight in Walden, turn right to stay on NY 208 North to Wallkill. At the stop sign, turn left on Wallkill Avenue; continue 0.2 mile and turn left onto Bruyn Turnpike/CR 18 (post office on corner). Drive 1.4 miles to Hoagerburgh Road; turn right. In 1.5 miles turn right into Shawangunk Grasslands National Wildlife Refuge. Trailhead GPS: N41 38.120' / W74 12.780'

THE HIKE

"It's just a big field!" noted a visitor who arrived at Shawangunk Grasslands when we did, demonstrating the difference in perspective between birders and non-birders. If you have the slightest interest in birds, you will see the benefits in preserving this truly glorious wildlife habitat in its natural state, even though this 597-acre national wildlife refuge actually is just a big, open field.

Preservation of grassland habitat for birds and other wildlife has become a high priority in the northeastern United States, where most open fields are used either for grazing livestock, growing animal feed like orchard grass and hay, or cultivating cash crops like corn and soybeans. While it may seem like farmers' fields would be ideal habitat for grassland birds, the truth is that nesting birds and farmland don't mix. Grassland birds build their nests and lay eggs in late May and early June, just as feed crops reach their healthful peak. Farmers must move quickly to mow and bale their hay to capture this

This open field provides critically important habitat for grassland birds and butterflies.

Many bobolinks nest in this refuge, singing about their territory throughout May and June.

nutritious feed—but this mowing destroys nests, as well as the hatched nestlings they may contain. Bobolinks, grasshopper sparrows, common grackles, red-winged blackbirds, eastern meadowlarks, and other grassland birds are usually too traumatized by the loss of their nests to attempt to renest in the same place (and some farmers reseed and mow again later in the summer). This unfortunate lack of symbiosis between birds and farmers has contributed significantly to the decline in these bird species observed by ornithologists over the last several decades.

A number of field researchers are working throughout the region to communicate this issue to farmers, and to suggest ways they can harvest their crops without destroying birds. While this effort continues, we can be grateful to the national wildlife refuge system for having the foresight to preserve this patch of grassland, and for the easy trails throughout the refuge that provide visitors with plenty of opportunity to observe birds as they raise their young.

Shawangunk Grasslands provides prime habitat for bobolinks, a bubbly-voiced black bird with a bright yellow patch on the back of the male's head, and white patches on its wings and back. Bobolink numbers have declined precipitously throughout its range in North America, enough so that Canada has placed the bird on its endangered species list. Here in Shawangunk Grasslands, however, bobolinks seem to be everywhere, perching on top of saplings or on sturdy plants and singing continuously. Eastern meadowlarks, unmistakable for their bright yellow throat and chest interrupted by a thick, black V, also breed here. You can spot them perched in small trees or on fences to whistle their clear, melodious song; a white patch on the tail makes them easy to identify in flight. Both of these birds nest close to or right on the ground, making them inevitable targets for harvesting equipment—but no mowing takes place during breeding season in this preserve, so the birds multiply safely. The symphony of birdsong here in late May and early June can be absolutely thrilling to birders and non-birders alike.

Just 0.2 mile down the blue-blazed trail from the parking area, visitors enjoy a rare treat: A large box on a post set back from the trail provides nesting for a pair of American kestrels, the continent's smallest and most brightly marked falcon. A trailside bench provides seating to watch the kestrels hunt for large insects like dragonflies and grasshoppers, small rodents, frogs, and occasional birds to carry to the nest box's opening, where they feed their nestlings and then take off to hunt once again. Kestrels have the unusual ability to hover in one place as they survey a field looking for prey, a fascinating feat to witness.

Shawangunk Grasslands also provides habitat for more common birds, including savannah sparrow, American goldfinch, Baltimore oriole, eastern bluebird, field sparrow, song sparrow, and upland sandpiper, a state-threatened species that has declined significantly in recent years. Grasshopper, vesper, and Henslow's sparrows are found here regularly—species that can be difficult to find in New York. Golden-winged and blue-winged warblers migrate through here in May on their way north, and a number of flycatchers make this grassland an annual stop as well. A winter visit can reveal short-eared owls, northern harriers, and rough-legged hawks soaring over the fields as they hunt for voles, shrews, and mice.

For gardeners and others with a more horticultural bent, Shawangunk Grasslands tests your knowledge of native plants with dozens of flowering species, grasses, and small trees. Several species of milkweed attract butterflies, including eastern tiger swallowtail, monarch, black swallowtail, orange sulphur, great spangled fritillary, red admiral, and meadow fritillary. Expect to find columbine, bergamot, and yarrow in spring; black-eyed Susan and coneflower in early summer; boneset, snakeroot, fleabane, daisy, and joe-pye weed in late summer; and goldenrods and asters for an end–of–summer finale.

Whose great idea was it to preserve this prime patch of Catskill acreage? Thank the US General Services Administration (GSA) for having

American kestrels use this nest box to raise young, hunting the grasslands for insects and rodents to feed their nestlings.

the foresight to transfer the former Galeville Army Airfield to the US Fish & Wildlife Service after the airfield closed in 1994. The land became a national wildlife refuge in

The trail is almost completely level, with several benches for rest stops.

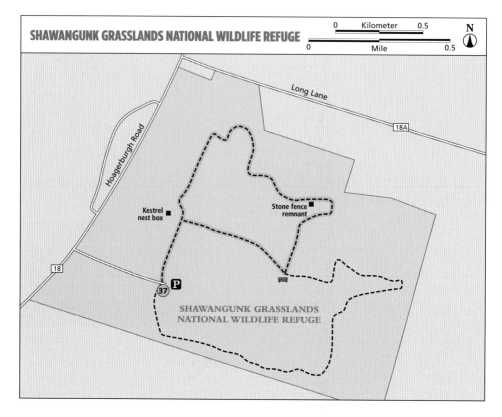

1999, including 55 acres the GSA gave to the town of Shawangunk for use as a park. Shawangunk Grasslands became the western boundary of the Shawangunk Valley habitat complex, which extends east to the Plattekill Hills. The airfield's runways translated nicely to trails throughout the refuge, and the management added a perimeter trail, part of which you will follow by taking the hike described below.

MILES AND DIRECTIONS

0.0 Start from the parking area and proceed north on the blue-blazed trail (Tabor Trace).

0.2 The red- and blue-blazed trails meet here. There's a bench here, as well as an American kestrel nest box to your left, some distance from the bench. This is a great place to view this falcon's nesting and breeding behavior in May and June. When you're ready, continue straight (northeast) on the blue-blazed trail.

1.1 The remains of a stone fence stand to the right of the trail. Continue straight and around the upcoming bend.

1.5 At the bench and the intersection with the red-blazed trail, turn right to complete the loop. (**Option:** You can add about 2.5 miles to your hike by continuing straight on the red-blazed trail, which also loops back to the parking area.)

2.0 You have reached the first intersection, at the bench near the kestrel box. Turn left to return to the parking area.

2.2 Arrive back at the parking area.

SOUTHWESTERN CATSKILLS

As we explore this last quadrant of Catskill Park, the hikes we have chosen focus as much on human endeavor as they do on lovely scenery. Here we encounter remnants of some of the region's most famous history, from a Revolutionary War battle to industrial production and transportation—and on to the twentieth century's largest and best-remembered rock concert.

Among these events and achievements, we still find some exquisite scenery, including the waterfall on Vernooy Kill, deep in the Sundown Wild Forest. The outskirts of Minnewaska State Park Preserve also offer us one more gorgeous view, at Sam's Point, and one mysterious cave that remains icy even at the height of summer—in fact, we explored it in July and had to watch our step on slick stone stairs.

The battle at Minisink may not have figured prominently in the annals of American history, but it sheds some light on an aspect of the war not discussed in big Broadway musicals: the neighbor-against-neighbor skirmishes that pitted British regulars against local militias. The history here also highlights the involvement of Native Americans on both sides of the conflict, some fooled by the British into thinking they were defending land they would continue to own after the war.

Walking along a length of the former Delaware and Hudson Canal reveals the story of one of many side canals that brought goods out of rural areas to the Hudson River, where boats laden with coal, tanned hides, or produce could proceed to New York City or go north to the Erie Canal. So little evidence remains of the Catskills as an industrial region that we found this hike particularly enlightening—and the old stone walls of various bits of canal structure, the abundant birds and wildflowers, and a glimpse of a bear all made this a delightful hike.

Finally, if you want to know more about the Summer of Love, the biggest rock concert of the 1960s, and what it meant to an entire generation, visit Bethel Woods Center for the Arts, tour the Woodstock Museum, and walk the Bindy Bazaar Trail. Nothing brings the enormity of this weekend in August 1969 to life like this lovingly designed, historically fascinating museum—and topping it off with a stroll through trees festooned with fiber art somehow brings the entire experience together. Woodstock put Sullivan County on the national map in a way the massive old resorts never did—and you have this opportunity to spend an afternoon feeling as if you were there.

38 MINNEWASKA STATE PARK PRESERVE: SAM'S POINT ROAD TO THE ICE CAVES

There's nothing like a naturally chilled cave on a hot summer day.

County: Ulster
Start: Parking lot in Sam's Point Area of Minnewaska State Park Preserve
Elevation gain: 200 feet
Distance: 3.6 miles out and back
Difficulty: Moderate
Hiking time: About 2.5 hours
Seasons: Spring through fall
Schedule: Open daily, 9 a.m. to closing (closing time posted at preserve entrance)
Fees and permits: Entrance fee per vehicle
Trail contact: Sam's Point Area of Minnewaska State Park Preserve, 400 Sam's Point Rd., Cragsmoor 12420; (845) 647-7989; parks.ny.gov/parks/127/details.aspx
Canine compatibility: Dogs permitted on leash, though the hike may be too difficult for dogs.
Trail surface: Gravel and pavement to the Ice Caves entrance, then uneven stone steps that may be wet and slippery; stone and dirt cave floor, wooden walkways and wood ladders

Land status: New York State Park Preserve
Nearest town: Walker Valley, New York (south); Ellenville, New York (north)
Other trail users: Hikers only
Maps: NatGeo TOPO! Map (USGS): Napanoch, NY; NatGeo Trails Illustrated Map #750: Shawangunk Mountains; New York–New Jersey Trail Conference Trail Map 104: Shawangunk Trails
Special considerations: The Ice Cave Trail contains ice flows (even in summer), water, uneven rock steps, narrow crevices, low rock ceilings, dark areas, ladders, and boardwalks. Use extreme caution on the trail through the cave. Wear boots with ankle support, and take your time on this trail. A walking stick may be helpful in getting down the steps. Call the office when planning a hike in spring, as the ice in the caves must melt sufficiently to allow safe passage before the trail is opened for the season.

FINDING THE TRAILHEAD

From Middletown, take NY 17 West to exit 113 for US 209. Take US 209 to NY 52 East and turn left. Continue 0.7 mile to Cragsmoor Road. Turn right onto Cragsmoor and follow it 1.5 miles. Turn right onto Sam's Point Road. The parking area is on the left, at 400 Sam's Point Road. Trailhead GPS: N41 40.217' / W74 21.651'

THE HIKE

This hike through a portion of Sam's Point Preserve, a unit of Minnewaska State Park Preserve, delivers a double treat—especially if you're trying to beat the heat. First, you can enjoy one of the most spectacular views available of the park and surrounding area from Sam's Point, a wide stone ledge (or a second, slightly higher ledge) that provides a 270-degree countryside panorama. Second, you can continue from the point to the Ice Caves, a labyrinth of staircases, corridors, squeezes, climbs, and wet spots that can include mounds of snow and slippery ice—even in the heat of July.

Sam's Point shares the geology of the Shawangunk Ridge.

The route through the Ice Caves has uneven stairs, aging railings, and lots of damp areas.

On a clear day, the view from Sam's Point seems endless.

The caves here are part of the Ellenville Fault, a fracture in the earth caused by the movement of the rock walls below, forcing them to break apart. Here in Minnewaska, the resulting open fault exposed the cave passages just enough to let in some light as well as rain and snow, but not enough to heat the chasm throughout the descent to the bottom. On the day we visited, the temperature inside the cave was as much as 30 degrees lower than at the surface, making for a very welcome respite from the summer heat.

So, who was Sam, and why does he have a point? The story goes that Sam, most likely a European-descended individual, managed to enrage the local Indians into chasing him through this particular area (probably in the 1700s, when tensions flared often between Native American tribes and new settlers). He reached the ledge and could either surrender—an unattractive concept that would certainly have led to his execution—or leap to his probable death. Sam chose the leap, and the fates smiled on him as he fell: The trees broke his fall, so he escaped the angry mob and probably suffered nothing worse that some scrapes and scratches. The ledge has borne his name ever since. Coming from the region that supplied us with legends including Rip Van Winkle and the Headless Horseman, the tale provides just enough truthfulness to satisfy curious visitors.

The road you will follow on your way to the cave was the work of the Civilian Conservation Corps (CCC), the workforce created by President Franklin D. Roosevelt to train unemployed, able-bodied young men in a wide range of trades during the Great Depression of the 1930s. CCC members built roads, constructed trails, and erected facilities in national and state parks across the United States, and many of them assisted in fighting fires in the parks as well. They constructed this road to provide access to the backcountry in case of a forest fire, and this particular road became a critical asset in 2016 when 2,028 acres of the Sam's Point Area burned for more than a week.

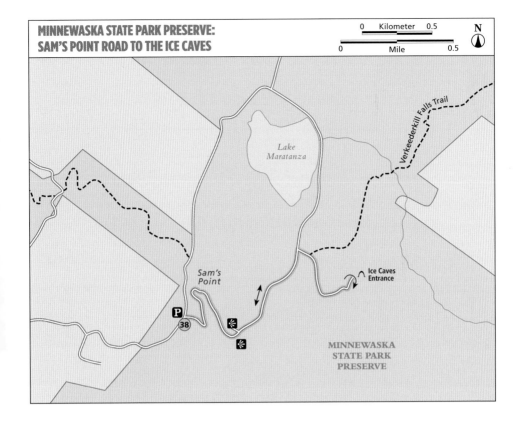

MINNEWASKA STATE PARK PRESERVE:
SAM'S POINT ROAD TO THE ICE CAVES

Lake
Maratanza

Verkeerderkill Falls Trail

Sam's
Point

Ice Caves
Entrance

P
38

MINNEWASKA
STATE PARK
PRESERVE

MILES AND DIRECTIONS

0.0 Start at the kiosk at the north end of the parking area and take the right-hand path toward the Ice Caves.

0.6 A large rock slab to your right offers a place to stand for a tremendous view of the surrounding area. This is the lower portion of Sam's Point.

0.7 A path to the left leads to the official Sam's Point, which is higher than the overlook you just passed.

1.1 Turn right here for the Ice Caves Trail (white blaze). The Loop Road continues straight ahead and loops around Lake Maratanza.

1.2 The Verkeerderkill Falls Trail begins here to the left. (**Note:** When we hiked this trail in 2017, Verkeerderkill Falls was closed because of a forest fire here in 2016.) As you come around the next bend on your way to the Ice Caves, watch for another great viewpoint.

1.5 Reach the entrance to the Ice Caves. The map from here is an approximate length and path, as GPS devices don't function underground. You will go down stone steps to the bottom, then through a narrow passage, across some boardwalk, up ladders, and probably through some icy or snowy sections.

2.0 Emerge from the cave a short distance from where you went in. Return to the parking area on the trail that got you here.

3.6 Arrive back at the parking area.

39 UPPER FALLS OF VERNOOY KILL

This "wedding cake" falls flows in the deep woods on the outskirts of Catskill Park.

County: Ulster
Start: The dead end of Trails End Road outside New Paltz, after it has become a dirt road. The yellow gate with the stop sign denotes the trail entrance.
Elevation gain: 305 feet
Distance: 2.0 miles out and back
Difficulty: Easy
Hiking time: About 1 hour
Seasons: Spring and fall
Schedule: Open daily, dawn to dusk
Fees and permits: No fees or permits required
Trail contact: NYSDEC Region 3, 21 South Putt Corners Rd., New Paltz

12561; (845) 256-3064; dec.ny.gov/lands/75346.html
Canine compatibility: Dogs permitted on leash
Trail surface: Dirt path with many rocks and roots
Land status: New York State Department of Environmental Conservation
Nearest town: Ellenville, New York
Other trail users: Snowmobiles, trail runners
Maps: DeLorme: New York State Atlas & Gazetteer: Page 102

FINDING THE TRAILHEAD

From Ellenville, take US 209 North to CR 3 (Samsonville Road). Turn left on CR 3 and in 3.4 miles bear left on Upper Cherry Town Road. Continue on Upper Cherry Town Road (past the parking area on this road) until it ends at Trails End Road. Turn left and drive on Trails End Road until it becomes a dirt road; continue on the dirt road until it ends at a parking area. You will see a yellow gate with a stop sign. This is the trailhead. Trailhead GPS: N41 53.050' / W74 21.635'

THE HIKE

Pick a warm spring day and walk this fairly easy trail to a many-faceted waterfall that probably receives far less than its fair share of visitors. The rocky path through the lush Sundown Wild Forest, a preserve tended by the New York State Department of Environmental Conservation, seems not as well-worn as many others we hiked for this book—perhaps because the path begins in a wilderness area far behind a sparse housing development. You need to pay attention while you're driving here, as lots of side roads and surface changes can confuse you and send you off in the wrong direction. Give it a try, however, because this falls and the surrounding preserve are well worth the trouble.

The trail through these woods is a multiuse path, so you may run into people on horseback in spring and summer, or on snowmobiles in winter. It's part of an 11.2-mile loop that begins in the tiny town of Rochester (not to be confused with the thriving metropolis of the same name on the shores of Lake Ontario) and passes through Balsam Swamp and over Vernooy Kill. (You will only see a mile of that length on this hike.) Like most trails in the Catskills, this one features many embedded rocks and some large

Upper Vernooy Kill flows through this wilderness area.

boulders. You may be distracted by small, furry animals, a white-tailed deer or two, and the occasional patch of wildflowers, so don't forget to watch your step.

The falls itself drops down a series of ledges stacked one on top of the other, spreading out toward the base to create the wedding-cake effect. One of these layers flows right under a bridge over Vernooy Kill (*kill* is the Dutch word for stream), and the widely

Top: The verdant woodland thrives along the river's edge.
Bottom: Upper Vernooy Kill Falls is one of the prettiest in the region.

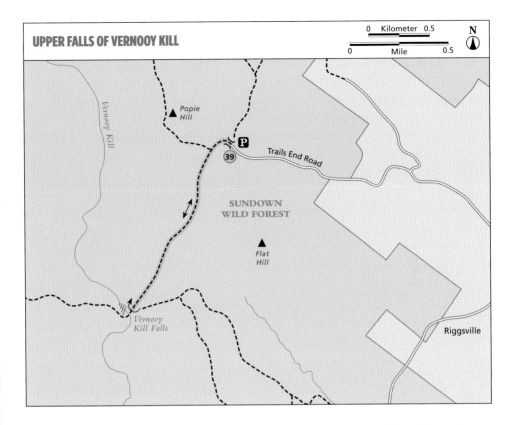

UPPER FALLS OF VERNOOY KILL

0 Kilometer 0.5
0 Mile 0.5
N

Vernooy Kill

Popie Hill

P

39 Trails End Road

SUNDOWN
WILD FOREST

Flat
Hill

Vernooy
Kill Falls

Riggsville

spaced boards on the bridge deck allow you to see the falls flowing directly beneath your feet. A quick walk along the kill brings you to the end of the falls' many short drops for an excellent view of the entire water feature from the bottom. Don't miss the stone wall along the stream, the last remains of the Vernooy Mill complex that harnessed the power of the kill and its falls from the early 1700s until 1809.

MILES AND DIRECTIONS

0.0 Start from the parking area at the end of Trails End Road and take the reddish-orange–marked path around the yellow gate with the stop sign. Cross a footbridge and follow the markers that say, "Snowmobile Trail." You can see bright blue trail markers and aqua blazes for the Long Trail on this path as well.

0.6 Cross through a wet area on the path. There's a second wet area coming up, just as you begin to hear the falls.

1.0 The trail goes right and left. Go left toward the falls. In a moment, reach a clearing where you'll see the trail registry. The bridge over the falls is in sight; walk out onto the bridge to see the falls. If you like, continue along the kill another 50 feet or so for more views of the falls. When you're ready, return on the path you followed to get here.

2.0 Arrive back at the parking area.

40 DELAWARE AND HUDSON CANAL LINEAR PARK TRAIL

Whether you seek a peaceful nature walk, a fitness trail, or a lesson in New York transportation history, this path delivers for you.

County: Sullivan
Start: Hornbeck's Basin parking area, 0.5 mile north of Wurtsboro at 3346 US 209
Elevation gain: 18 feet
Distance: 3.5 miles as a shuttle hike; 7.0 miles out and back
Difficulty: Moderate due to length
Hiking time: About 2 hours one way, 3.5 hours round-trip
Seasons: Year-round
Schedule: Open daily, 8 a.m. to dusk
Fees and permits: No fees or permits required
Trail contact: Sullivan County Parks and Recreation; (845) 794-3000; sullivanny.us

Canine compatibility: Dogs permitted on leash
Trail surface: Crushed stone
Land status: Managed by Sullivan County
Nearest town: Wurtsboro, Summitville, Phillipsport, New York
Other trail users: Anglers, bicyclists, joggers, trail runners; cross-country skiers, snowshoers (in season)
Maps: Trail Keeper D&H Canal Linear Trail (trailkeeper.org/trail/d-h-canal-linear-trail-wurtsboro-to-phillipsport/)

FINDING THE TRAILHEAD

From I-84, take exit 19B for NY 17 West toward Binghamton. Continue 13 miles to exit 113 for US 209/Wurtsboro and Ellenville. Take the exit, and turn right on US 209 North. In 2.1 miles, turn right into the Hornbeck's Basin parking area. Trailhead GPS: N41 58.602' / W74 47.432'

THE HIKE

Visitors and residents of Sullivan County are the happy beneficiaries of the Delaware & Hudson (D&H) Canal Linear Park, a 5.0-mile walking trail with adjoining parkland and historical exhibits that tell an important Catskills story. Here from the late 1820s through the end of that century, the D&H Canal provided the only shipping lane for anthracite coal mined in northeastern Pennsylvania to reach buyers along the Hudson River.

The D&H Canal partnered with the Pennsylvania Coal Company to become part of a complex shipping system that began across New York State's southern border, linking with 16 miles of gravity railway constructed by the coal company. When anthracite completed its rail journey to Honesdale, New York, it was loaded onto barges that made their way through 108 locks in 108 miles, paralleling the Lackawaxen and Delaware Rivers in succession until the canal reached Port Jervis. From here it turned to the east, making its way to the Hudson River by following the Neversink and Rondout Creeks. When the coal reached Rondout, workers unloaded it from the canal boats and reloaded it onto steamships, which traveled the Hudson River to bring the material to markets in New York City.

D&H Canal Linear Park crosses through neighborhoods between Phillipsport and Wurtsboro.

This laborious journey must have been very lucrative for the coal companies for them to endure this much time and effort. It took the coal seven to ten days to complete the journey, traveling the canal at 1 to 3 miles per hour on barges pulled by mules. Traveling by water was the only way to transport the coal for long distances, however, so despite all manner of obstacles—a cholera epidemic, unstable and seeping canal banks, competition from other canals in the area, and the ups and downs of the national economy—the D&H Canal Corporation became one of the largest private businesses in the country. Over time, the demand for coal led the canal owners to dig the waterway deeper to accommodate larger and heavier boats that could haul up to 140 tons of anthracite. This eliminated the need to transfer the load to steamships at the Hudson River, as these larger boats could go directly from the canal to the river and continue to New York City.

Trekking coal through the Catskills became much more than an industrial enterprise. Towns sprang up along the route to provide services to the boatmen and their families, who usually worked long days together keeping the load on track. Immigrants from Ireland and Germany populated the area as they worked to enlarge the canal, enriching the strong Dutch, English, and Native American area with new customs and culture. In addition to coal, industries already established in the region took advantage of the shipping opportunities for their own products, so lumber, paper, stone, cement, and tanned leathers also traversed the route to the Hudson.

So it went through the 1870s, until a new development in transportation came to the fore. Railroads quickly supplanted canals—locomotives could pull heavier loads and travel at faster speeds than boats powered by mules. Soon the Ontario and Western Railroad followed the D&H Canal's route, bringing coal to market more quickly and building routes into more communities to the north and west. Trains had the added advantage of functioning year-round, while the canal had to close down entirely for at least three

The mowed grass path follows the former towpath alongside the restored canal.

months during the winter. By the end of the 1890s, just 387 canal boats still traveled the water route; on November 5, 1898, the last coal boat completed the route at Rondout and pulled into dry dock. The D&H Canal had reached its end.

The D&H Canal Corporation opened all the locks and drained the canal in 1899, and simply abandoned it, allowing it to fill in with weeds and debris. Its demise struck a terrible blow to the communities along its length, especially those serving the shipping industry. Businesses that repaired boats or provided services to boatmen and their families closed their doors, and many towns stood empty as people moved away to seek their fortunes elsewhere. Railroads brought the need for new kinds of services, transporting hundreds of tourists every day into the fresh air and stunning scenery of the Catskill region, so the area filled with resorts and tour companies, transforming itself for a new era. The D&H Canal's remains stood nearly forgotten as the area changed with the times.

In 1969, Sullivan County acquired a small section of the canal's old route, including four locks that remained relatively intact. This parcel grew in 1986 when Orange and Rockland Counties donated 43 additional acres, providing enough land for the development of a linear park. With grant money from multiple sources, Sullivan County expanded the park to 83 acres, including five locks and a dry dock, and developed a trail with interpretive displays, picnic areas, parking, and comfort stations. Visitors can view the remains of the Boothroyd dry dock, an impressive stone structure where boats got the repairs they needed to continue to move their heavy loads; learn about the role that waste weirs played in maintaining a consistent water level throughout the canal; see basins and sluiceways that aided in canal water regulation and control; and see remnants of the original Lock 50, positioned at the beginning of the descent to the Hudson River.

Whether you have a passion for canal history or just want to take a nice walk through some peaceful neighborhoods and woodlands, you will find this uncommonly pleasant trail to your liking.

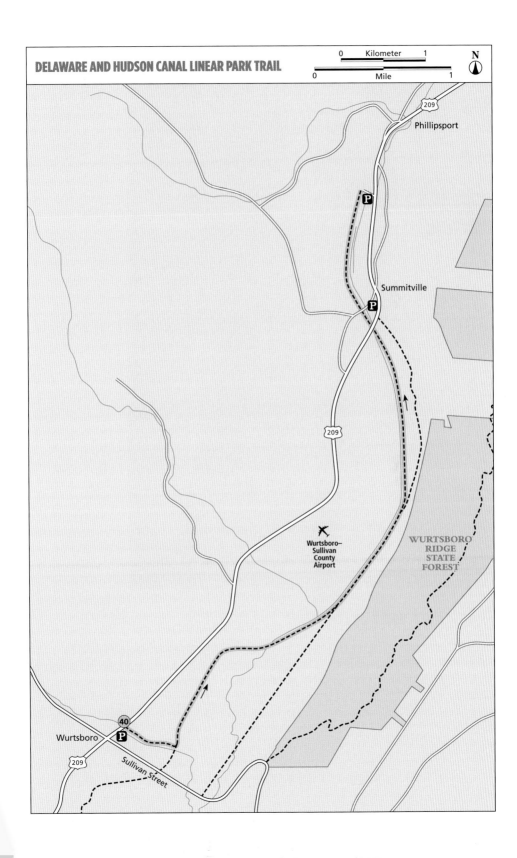

DELAWARE AND HUDSON CANAL LINEAR PARK TRAIL

Kilometer

Mile

N

209

Phillipsport

P

Summitville

P

209

✈
Wurtsboro–
Sullivan
County
Airport

WURTSBORO
RIDGE
STATE
FOREST

40

Wurtsboro

P

209

Sullivan Street

At the site of Lock 50, you can see remnants of structures nearly two centuries old.

MILES AND DIRECTIONS

0.0 Start on the trail, east of the parking area, and head east (turn left as you face the trail).

3.0 Reach the Summitville parking area at the "O&W Y Turn," part of the New York, Ontario and Western Railway. Continue straight.

3.5 Reach the Bova Road access point, where the D&H Canal Linear Park Interpretive Center is located. You can see waste weirs, dry docks, and other remnants of the canal's heyday just off the trail here. This is a convenient place to end your hike, as you can park a second car here to shuttle back to the beginning. The trail does continue north to join the NY O&W Rail Trail from here. (*Option:* If you did not park an additional vehicle here, this is a good turnaround point. Return to Wurtsboro the way you came for a 7.0-mile hike.)

41 BETHEL WOODS BINDY BAZAAR TRAIL

You know you want to—so do it! Get groovy and visit the site of the historic 1969 Woodstock festival.

County: Sullivan
Start: Front of the entrance to the Museum at Bethel Woods, at the signpost for the Bindy Bazaar Trail
Elevation gain: 84 feet
Distance: 1.2-mile lollipop
Difficulty: Easy
Hiking time: About 1 hour
Seasons: Spring through fall
Schedule: Grounds open daily, Apr 3 through Dec 31, 10 a.m. to 5 p.m.; closed in winter
Fees and permits: There is no charge to walk the grounds, but you really should spend some time in the museum (2022 rates: Adults $19.69, seniors $17, youth 6–18 $10, no charge for children under 5). Discounts for purchasing tickets online (recommended, especially in peak seasons).
Trail contact: Bethel Woods Center for the Arts; (845) 583-2000, bethelwoodscenter.org
Canine compatibility: Service animals only in the museum; leashed dogs welcome on trails
Trail surface: Pavement and groomed woodland paths
Land status: Owned by the Bethel Woods Center for the Arts
Nearest town: Bethel, New York
Other trail users: Tourists and museum visitors
Maps: Bethel Woods Center (bethelwoodscenter.org/sites/default/files/bwca-groundmap-2018New2-edit020620-01.png)

FINDING THE TRAILHEAD

From I-87 (New York State Thruway), take exit 16 to Harriman. Merge onto NY 18 and continue to exit 104 for NY 17B. In about 10 miles, turn right onto Hurd Road at the sign for Bethel Woods. Continue to the parking area. Trailhead GPS: N41 41.816' / W74 52.195'

THE HIKE

On August 15, 1969, more than 400,000 people gathered on Max Yasgur's dairy farm in Bethel, in New York's Catskill region—no, not in the nearby town of Woodstock—for "an Aquarian Exposition: 3 Days of Peace and Music," according to the organizers' advertising. Joel Rosenman and John P. Roberts, two relatively inexperienced New York City entrepreneurs, joined forces with attorneys Michael Lang and Artie Kornfeld to form Woodstock Ventures, a promotional company that put together the concert. That organization gave the event its name, and today Woodstock remains a pinnacle in rock festival history.

Why does Woodstock stand alone as a festival achievement more than half a century later, especially in our current era, which features massive events like Coachella and Burning Man? First, the band lineup remains extraordinary: Richie Havens, The Band, with Levon Helm on lead vocals and drums; Arlo Guthrie; Joan Baez; Santana; John Sebastian; the Grateful Dead; Creedence Clearwater Revival; Janis Joplin; Sly and the Family Stone; Melanie; The Who; Jefferson Airplane; Joe Cocker; Blood, Sweat & Tears; Crosby, Stills, Nash & Young; and Jimi Hendrix, among others. Second, the majority of

The trailhead for the Bindy Bazaar Trail is clearly marked and easy to see.

the audience got in for free—more by circumstance than by intention, as the promoters found they could not assemble barriers around Yasgur's field or place ticket booths in the limited time they had before the event. While 186,000 tickets were sold in advance at $18 each, so many attendees arrived at the same time in the little town of Bethel that they swarmed the farm, making any organized ticket collection process impossible.

Woodstock's enduring legacy, however, comes from the atmosphere of peace and love among the audience, especially at a festival so overrun with attendees that they overwhelmed the limited sanitation and first-aid facilities and depleted the food supplies the organizers provided in a single night. Despite rain, mud, and rampant marijuana and hallucinogenic drug use, only a handful of minor crimes were reported by the massive security force. Roberts received a call from New York Governor Nelson Rockefeller on Sunday, August 17, offering to send a 10,000-troop National Guard detail, but Roberts turned him down, noting that peace had prevailed up to that point and was likely to continue. Indeed, he was right: The sense of good-natured fun lasted straight through Hendrix's iconic rendition of "The Star Spangled Banner," a performance that became a touchstone for the '60s generation and beyond.

How can you get a sense of this remarkable event, and grasp what it meant to the people who participated? Start with a visit to the Museum at Bethel Woods, where interactive exhibits, videos, sound clips, and memorabilia combine to create a nostalgic sensory experience of the festival and its music. The museum also provides an understanding of Woodstock in context, with displays and video that capture the turmoil of 1969 leading up to the concert, and Woodstock's effect on the American zeitgeist years after it was over.

When you are filled with wonder at the event's scope and lasting influence, take a walk on the Bindy Bazaar Trail. The Bindy Bazaar, constructed during the Woodstock festival in the "magic forest" on Yasgur's property, housed twenty or so booths of arts and crafts,

Stop at the Woodstock Monument to view the site of the 1969 music event.

clothing, head shop paraphernalia, and other wares for sale by vendors. A few historic photos portray the bazaar as a colorful marketplace, draped in tie-dyed, painted, and embroidered tapestries and filled with imaginative handmade goods. Some people came to the bazaar simply to take a break from the crowds in the main field, wandering and finding themselves in a bright, fragrant environment. Others bought items that would remind them of the festival for decades to come.

Organizers of the bazaar denoted the layout of the booths in the woods by placing stones at the corners of each booth. These stones remain in the same places fifty-plus years later, and replicas of the pathway signposts have been placed on the same trees that sported them in 1969. The colorful booths themselves were dismantled at the end of the festival, but the Museum at Bethel Woods came up with a fascinating way to recall the spirit of the bazaar: a public art installation of crocheted textiles, created to wrap around the trees and remain in place throughout the seasons. Artist Carol Hummel spent untold hours on this outdoor exhibition, and the result is unlike anything you will see anywhere else, emphasizing "the use of textile and color celebrated in the era, juxtaposed with a technique unique and representative of contemporary times," notes the Bethel Woods Center for the Arts website. You can wander around in these woods and discover all of the snappily dressed trees along restored trails, as well as on some trails not yet fully redeveloped; the trail system expansion is ongoing.

On your way to the Bindy Bazaar, the path takes you to the Woodstock Monument, which overlooks the location of the main stage and the field where the concert took place. The festival site landed on the National Register of Historic Places in 2017, acknowledging the importance of the farm and the event that happened here. This means the festival site will stay in its current condition in perpetuity, protected by the National Park Service, which oversees the National Register.

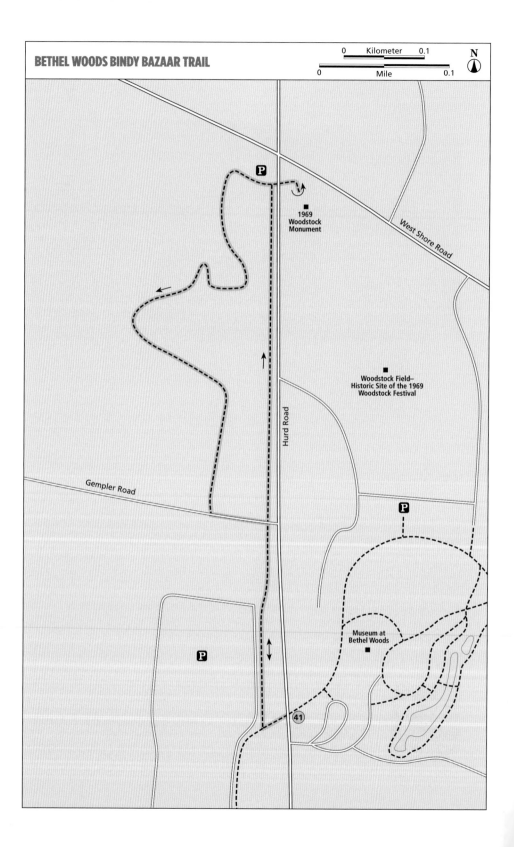

BETHEL WOODS BINDY BAZAAR TRAIL

0   Kilometer   0.1

0   Mile   0.1

N

West Shore Road

P

■
1969
Woodstock
Monument

■
Woodstock Field–
Historic Site of the 1969
Woodstock Festival

Hurd Road

Gempler Road

P

P

Museum at
Bethel Woods
■

P

41

MILES AND DIRECTIONS

0.0 Start at the sign for the Bindy Bazaar Trail on the walkway to the museum entrance in parking lot C. Follow the paved path to a mowed-grass path that passes between two split-rail fences. Follow the signs to the restored Bindy Bazaar Trails. The mowed-grass path soon becomes crushed stone.

0.3 At the four-way intersection, continue straight and bear right toward the Woodstock Festival Monument.

0.4 Arrive at the monument. When you are ready, return to the intersection and cross the road

0.6 Turn left on the gravel path.

0.7 When you see a tree covered in a crocheted pattern, enter the Bindy Bazaar Trail. Turn right and follow the trail into the woods. Wander as you like through the trees dressed in crocheted sweaters and other yarn designs. Eventually the path leads to the south entrance/exit for the woods. Pass through this and out of the woods, and continue on the path to close the loop back at the parking area.

1.2 Arrive back at the museum entrance.

Trail signs within the woods are replicas of the handmade signs posted by vendors at the 1969 festival.

Carol Hummel's textile art creates an impression of the colors and crafts sold in the original Bindy Bazaar.

42 MINISINK BATTLEGROUND PARK

This shady natural area once erupted in battle between British and American troops and the Mohawk Indians.

County: Sullivan
Start: Parking area at the Minisink Battleground Interpretive Center. The trail begins west of parking, on the park road (look for the gate).
Elevation gain: 151 feet
Distance: 0.7-mile loop
Difficulty: Easy
Hiking time: About 45 minutes
Seasons: Spring through fall
Schedule: Open daily 8 a.m. to dusk
Fees and permits: No fees or permits required
Trail contact: Sullivan County Parks and Recreation, 100 North St.,
Monticello 12701; (845) 794-3000; co .sullivan.ny.us
Canine compatibility: Dogs permitted on leash
Trail surface: Dirt, rocks, and forest detritus
Land status: Sullivan County park
Nearest town: Lackawaxen, Pennsylvania
Other trail users: Hikers only
Maps: Orientation map available online at minisink.org/minisink battlemap.jpg

FINDING THE TRAILHEAD

From NY 97 at the Roebling Bridge, head north on CR 168, following the signs to Minisink Battleground Park. The park entrance will be on your left. From the parking area, look west for the gate on the park road. This is the trailhead. Trailhead GPS: N41 29.277' / W74 58.195'

THE HIKE

This little gem of a park is within the boundaries of the Upper Delaware Scenic and Recreational River, an area preserved by the National Park Service for its historical and natural value. Minisink Battleground is managed by Sullivan County, but, like so many properties within national park boundaries that maintain their local oversight, it benefits from the park service's supervision as well as the involvement of passionate local professionals and volunteers.

With all that we know about the Revolutionary War and the lines of men in red coats facing lines of men in blue and homespun on the formal field of battle, another kind of battle receives less attention until we visit a place like Minisink Battleground. Here there were no regiments kneeling with muskets in uniform lines—instead, this battle came at the end of a long series of raids carried out on villages by mixed parties of Mohawk Indians and British soldiers led by Col. Joseph Brant.

A Mohawk warrior with a degree from Dartmouth College and a lifelong resident of this general area, Brant led the Indians who had thrown in their lot with the British Loyalists when the war began, believing that the outcome would favor the English and that their land would be returned to them once the conflict ended. Over the course of several days, Brant and his warring party tore through the Neversink Valley, torching buildings and farms, stealing cattle and horses, and leaving little for the families who populated the area.

Indian Rock honors the Iroquois who died at Minisink.

The American militia came together quickly to retaliate and attempt to stop the marauders, forming two groups led by Lt. Col. Benjamin Tusten, a medical doctor, and Maj. Samuel Meeker from New Jersey. They moved up the river behind the Brant contingent, planning a surprise attack to recover the settlers' belongings and cattle rather than to make war. Soon a militia led by Col. John Hathorn joined the two bands on the move, bringing the total number of men at arms to roughly 120.

At Hospital Rock, an American doctor and seventeen wounded soldiers lost their lives in an Iroquois and British attack.

On July 22, 1779, the militias realized that Brant and his men were coming across the Delaware River at Lackawaxen, and they made ready to ambush the Mohawk and British. Moments before they would make their move, however, one of the Americans fired a shot—perhaps accidentally, perhaps on purpose—and alerted Brant to their location. In short order, Brant and his men moved to surround the militias on the hill that is now Minisink Battleground Park, cutting one militia off from the other two and causing panic among the Patriots. The remaining forty-five or fifty Americans attempted a rush up the hill to gain the high ground, forming a defensive square and battling valiantly to hold their own. Their strategy—or perhaps their lack of one—finally gave way, however, as Brant and his men scattered the square and killed the men who remained. By day's end, as many as fifty Americans had died in the battle, while only seven of Brant's men succumbed.

As you walk the well-groomed trail here, keep in mind that it's hard to pinpoint exactly where most of the battle took place, as there were no structures or earthworks constructed and only a handful of landmarks remain. The named rocks help give the battleground some definition: Sentinel Rock, from which Brant made his final attack through the defensive square; Hospital Rock, where Tusten and seventeen wounded men found themselves trapped; and Indian Rock, where legend has it that Brant buried his dead warriors (though no one has ever found evidence of this).

Your walk along the Battleground Trail takes you through the story of a Revolutionary War battle with a cast of characters who are not household names outside of this local area—but who were critical to the fight for and against independence in southern

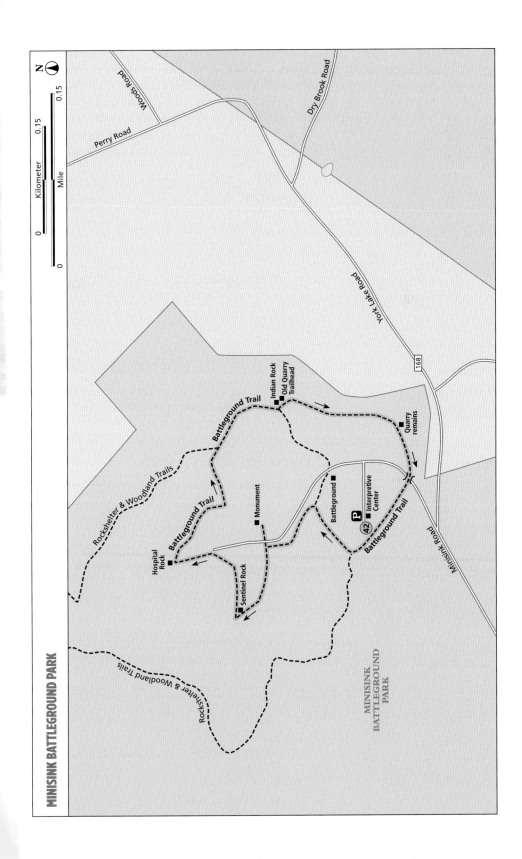

MINISINK BATTLEGROUND PARK

N

Kilometer
0   0.15   0.15

Mile
0   0.15

Perry Road

Woods Road

Dry Brook Road

York Lake Road

168

Battleground Trail

Indian Rock
Old Quarry Trailhead

Quarry remains

Rockshelter & Woodland Trails

Battleground Trail

Monument

Hospital Rock

Battleground

Interpretive Center

P
42

Battleground Trail

Sentinel Rock

Minisink Road

Rockshelter & Woodland Trails

MINISINK BATTLEGROUND PARK

New York. Here you will learn about the Mohawks' loyalty to the British rather than the new Americans—unlike other tribes of the Iroquois Confederacy—and about the men who fought and died on both sides in the bloody battle. The last part of this hike passes through an area that supplied bluestone—a popular and highly valued paving and foundation stone—to much of the eastern United States in the early days of the new country.

We found something particularly delightful in this park: natural quiet, a commodity that has become hard to find anywhere in the densely populated and well-traveled state. Here you can hear yourself think, pick out the songs of various warblers and vireos in spring and early summer, and enjoy the rustling of leaves as squirrels, chipmunks, and robins make their way along the forest floor. While the noise from NY 97 is only a mile or so away, the geography helps keep the traffic noise at bay so you can enjoy a bit of a wilderness experience.

MILES AND DIRECTIONS

0.0 Start at the gate on the park road, west of the parking area. Proceed past the gate and turn left onto the Battleground Trail.

0.1 At the top of the hill, follow the Battleground Trail to the left. A presentation area here includes a monument dedicated in 1879 on the one-hundredth anniversary of the battle.

0.2 Come to Sentinel Rock, in the southwest corner of the square occupied by the American defense. This is the top of Rocky Hill. In another few feet, the Woodland Trail goes left. Continue straight.

0.3 Reach Hospital Rock, where Dr. Benjamin Tusten, who was a lieutenant colonel in the American army, gave medical attention to seventeen wounded soldiers. All these Americans were trapped and killed at this rock by British and Mohawk soldiers.

0.4 At the junction with the Rockshelter and Woodland Trails, continue straight on the Battleground Trail.

0.5 At Indian Rock, the Old Quarry Trail goes left. Turn left here to extend your walk. (**Option:** Continue straight for a quick return to the parking area.)

0.6 On the Old Quarry Trail, you can see sheer rock walls along the mossy dike. At the intersection, go right to return to the parking area.

0.7 Arrive back at the parking area.

BONUS HIKES

There are miles and miles of trails across Catskill Park, many of which are extremely popular with hikers coming north from the New York City metro area. So far in this book, we've provided detailed information about some of the most well-traveled as well as some lesser-known trails we're sure you'll enjoy. This book is like a tasting menu—a sampling of some of the Catskill region's most spectacular and fascinating places—so you can decide where you'd like to explore further.

We want to be sure you can find your way to a variety of trails—from easy walks to strenuous, challenging hikes—in the Catskills as well as those trails in the shadow of this spectacular New York State treasure. Here are eight more hikes to entice you to explore this truly awe-inspiring part of the United States.

BALSAM LAKE MOUNTAIN AND FIRE TOWER

County: Delaware
Start: Dry Brook Ridge trailhead, 7176 Mill Brook Rd., Margaretville
Elevation gain: 1,204 feet
Distance: 5.9 miles out and back
Difficulty: Moderate
Hiking time: About 3.25 hours
Seasons: Year-round
Schedule: Open daily. Camping areas available.
Fees and permits: No fees or permits required
Trail contact: DEC Region 3 New Paltz Office; (845) 256-3076; email: r3forestry@dec.ny.gov

Canine compatibility: Dogs permitted on leash
Trail surface: Rocks, old woods road
Land status: New York State DEC Forest Preserve
Nearest town: Phoenicia, New York
Other trail users: Campers; snowshoers, cross-country skiers (in season)
Special considerations: Stay on the marked footpath; the first few miles of the trail cross private property.

HUGGINS LAKE

County: Delaware
Start: Berry Brook Road trailhead
Elevation gain: 912 feet
Distance: 4.4 miles out and back
Difficulty: Easy
Hiking time: About 1.75 hours
Seasons: Year-round
Schedule: Open daily. Camping areas available.
Fees and permits: No fees or permits required
Trail contact: DEC Region 4 Stamford Office (Mon through Fri, 8:30 a.m. to 4:30 p.m.); (607) 652-7365; email: r4.ump@dec.ny.gov

Canine compatibility: Dogs permitted on leash.
Trail surface: Old dirt road
Land status: New York State DEC Forest Preserve
Nearest town: Liberty, New York
Other trail users: Birders, campers; snowshoers (in season)
Special considerations: The path around the lake may not be well maintained. This is a good hike if you're camping at Beaverkill State Campground.

INDIAN HEAD MOUNTAIN LOOP

County: Greene
Start: Prediger Road trailhead
Elevation gain: 1,656 feet
Distance: 6.25-mile loop
Difficulty: Difficult, strenuous
Hiking time: 4 to 5 hours
Seasons: Year-round
Schedule: Open daily. Camping areas available.
Fees and permits: No fees or permits required
Trail contact: DEC Region 4 Stamford Office (Mon through Fri, 8:30 a.m. to 4:30 p.m.); (607) 652-7365; email: r4.ump@dec.ny.gov
Canine compatibility: Dogs permitted on leash
Trail surface: Roots, rocks
Land status: New York State DEC Forest Preserve
Nearest town: Tannersville, New York
Other trail users: Campers
Special considerations: There are some nearly vertical climbs on this hike.

SPLIT ROCK LOOKOUT

County: Delaware
Start: Holliday/Berry Brook Road
Elevation gain: 600 feet
Distance: 2.4 miles out and back
Difficulty: Moderate
Hiking time: About 2 hours
Seasons: Year-round
Schedule: Open daily. Camping areas available.
Fees and permits: No fees or permits required
Trail contact: DEC Region 5 Ray Brook Office; (518) 897-1200; email: info.r5@dec.ny.gov
Canine compatibility: Dogs permitted on leash
Trail surface: Dirt, roots, rocks, soft woods and bark
Land status: New York State DEC Forest Preserve
Nearest town: Roscoe, New York
Other trail users: Snowshoers (in season)
Special considerations: The first part of this trail crosses private land. Stay on the trail. The trail can be slippery on the steeper inclines, and the overlook can be a bit dangerous.

TANBARK LOOP

County: Ulster
Start: 8 Ava Maria Dr. and Ursula Place, Phoenicia. There is no parking lot. Cross Parish Field in Phoenicia Park to find the trailhead.
Elevation gain: 620 feet
Distance: 2.3-mile lollipop
Difficulty: Moderate, with some steep sections
Hiking time: About 1.5 hours
Seasons: Year-round
Schedule: Open daily. Camping areas available.
Fees and permits: No fees or permits required
Trail contact: DEC Region 3 New Paltz Office; (845) 256-3076; email: r3forestry@dec.ny.gov
Canine compatibility: Dogs permitted on leash
Trail surface: Roots, rocks, loose gravel
Land status: New York State DEC Forest Preserve
Nearest town: Phoenicia, New York
Other trail users: Runners
Special considerations: In summertime, there may be rattlesnakes on this hike.

THOMAS COLE MOUNTAIN

County: Greene
Start: Elmer Barnum Road parking area
Elevation gain: 2,148 feet
Distance: 5.8 miles out and back
Difficulty: Difficult, strenuous
Hiking time: About 4 hours
Seasons: Year-round
Schedule: Open daily; camping areas available
Fees and permits: No fees or permits required
Trail contact: DEC Region 4 Stamford Office (Mon through Fri, 8:30 a.m. to 4:30 p.m.); (607) 652-7365; email: r4.ump@dec.ny.gov

Canine compatibility: Dogs permitted on leash
Trail surface: Roots, rocks
Land status: New York State DEC Forest Preserve
Nearest town: Tannersville, New York
Other trail users: Campers; snowshoers (in season)
Special considerations: This hike is often done in conjunction with Black Dome and Blackhead Mountains. If you're interested in racking up the 3,500 peaks, you could grab three in one day. Bring a second vehicle and park it at the Big Hollow Road trailhead.

TROUT POND LOOP

County: Sullivan
Start: Russell Brook Road, Roscoe
Elevation gain: 1,660 feet
Distance: 4.9-mile loop
Difficulty: Easy
Hiking time: About 2.5 hours
Seasons: Year-round
Schedule: Open daily; camping areas available
Fees and permits: No fees or permits required
Trail contact: DEC Region 4 Stamford Office (Mon through Fri, 8:30 a.m. to 4:30 p.m.); (607) 652-7365; email: r4.ump@dec.ny.gov
Canine compatibility: Dogs permitted on leash
Trail surface: Roots, rocks, soft woods and bark
Land status: New York State DEC Forest Preserve
Nearest town: Roscoe, New York
Other trail users: Campers; snowmobilers (in season)
Special considerations: You can combine this with the Mud Pond Loop, which on its own is 4.5 miles.

HIKE INDEX

THE TEN ESSENTIALS OF HIKING

American Hiking Society

American Hiking Society recommends you pack the "Ten Essentials" every time you head out for a hike. Whether you plan to be gone for a couple of hours or several months, make sure to pack these items. Become familiar with these items and know how to use them.

1. Appropriate Footwear
Happy feet make for pleasant hiking. Think about traction, support, and protection when selecting well-fitting shoes or boots.

2. Navigation
While phones and GPS units are handy, they aren't always reliable in the backcountry; consider carrying a paper map and compass as a backup and know how to use them.

3. Water (and a way to purify it)
As a guideline, plan for half a liter of water per hour in moderate temperatures/terrain. Carry enough water for your trip and know where and how to treat water while you're out on the trail.

4. Food
Pack calorie-dense foods to help fuel your hike, and carry an extra portion in case you are out longer than expected.

5. Rain Gear & Dry-Fast Layers
The weatherman is not always right. Dress in layers to adjust to changing weather and activity levels. Wear moisture-wicking cloths and carry a warm hat.

6. Safety Items (light, fire, and a whistle)
Have means to start an emergency fire, signal for help, and see the trail and your map in the dark.

7. First Aid Kit

Supplies to treat illness or injury are only as helpful as your knowledge of how to use them. Take a class to gain the skills needed to administer first aid and CPR.

8. Knife or Multi-Tool

With countless uses, a multi-tool can help with gear repair and first aid.

9. Sun Protection

Sunscreen, sunglasses, and sun-protective clothing should be used in every season regardless of temperature or cloud cover.

10. Shelter

Protection from the elements in the event you are injured or stranded is necessary. A lightweight, inexpensive space blanket is a great option.

Find other helpful resources at AmericanHiking.org/hiking-resources